SenseAbilities

Understanding Sensory Integration

by

Maryann Colby Trott, M.A.

with

Marci K. Laurel, M.A., CCC-SLP, and
Susan L. Windeck, M.S., OTR/L

Illustrations based on photographs by Kirby Soderberg
Illustrations drawn under contract by Corwyn Zimbleman

pro·ed
An International Publisher

8700 Shoal Creek Boulevard
Austin, Texas 78757-6897
800/897-3202   Fax 800/397-7633
www.proedinc.com

© 1993 by Albuquerque Therapy Services
Published by PRO-ED, Inc.
8700 Shoal Creek Boulevard
Austin, Texas 78757-6897
800/897-3202   Fax 800/397-7633
www.proedinc.com

ISBN-13: 978-141640323-4
ISBN-10: 1-41640323-X

Previously published by Therapy Skill Builders, a division of The Psychological Corporation,
under ISBN 0761684387.

Printed in the United States of America

3   4   5   10   09   08

Dedication

For my parents,
who taught me with wisdom born of love.

For my children,
who lead me in paths of wonder.

For my husband,
who gives joy to the journey
and travels so faithfully beside me.

Acknowledgments

Many individuals have contributed to the completion of this book. The children that have been in my classrooms have given at least as much to me as I have to them. I am grateful for their patience and special brand of wisdom and humor. The outstanding staff of Albuquerque Therapy Services as well as other professionals with whom I have had the pleasure of working have contributed much of their considerable knowledge and experience as well as time, patience, and understanding. Special thanks to occupational therapists Mary Sue Williams, Jeanne DuRivage, Carla Cay Niemeyer, Sherry Shellenberger, and Kathy Taylor; OT assistants Lynn Anaya and Hillary Phelps; physical therapists Donna Cizmadia and Diana Kane-Hunnicutt; speech and language pathologist Mary Hartley; teachers Alice Maechtlen, Cathy Leppelman, Sharon Lessly, and Sarah Bieniarz; diagnostician Mary Pat Rael-Jones; and counselor Judy Lay. Patti Oetter was particularly generous in sharing her vast knowledge as well as valuable criticism and praise. Kirby Soderberg's patience, sensitivity, and creativity are expressed through the beauty of the children captured in his photographs. This book would be incomplete without the significant contributions, assistance, and encouragement of Sue Windeck and Marci Laurel. I appreciate the invaluable help of each person as well as the blessings of their continuing friendship.

Finally, thanks to my husband, Wayne, and the rest of my family with whom my life has been so richly blessed. The unconditional love and support that I receive from him and from my precious mother and friend, Dolores, constantly encourage me to find the things that lie within myself.

About the Authors

Maryann Colby Trott, M.A., is the leader of the Albuquerque Public Schools Developmental Disabilities Behavior Intervention Team and an educational consultant for Albuquerque Therapy Services. She has taught special education in the public schools since 1974. She has given numerous presentations on dealing with children with sensory integration disorders in the classroom and has published articles on teaching children with mental retardation.

Ms. Trott received her B.A. and M.A. in special education from the University of New Mexico in 1974 and 1981, respectively.

Marci K. Laurel, M.A., CCC-SLP, is a training coordinator and speech and language specialist at the University of New Mexico School of Medicine. She has worked as a speech pathologist for the past ten years and has given presentations and held workshops on language disorders and development in children. Ms. Laurel has been involved in exploring the relationships between sensory integration, speech and language, and learning, and has developed techniques for using the interrelationships among the three in therapy. She has also developed training programs for parents who have children with speech disorders and has served as director of a parent training program.

Ms. Laurel received a B.A. in speech pathology and audiology in 1980, and an M.A. in speech pathology in 1981. She received both degrees from the University of Florida at Gainesville.

Susan Lee Windeck, M.S., OTR/L, is president and chief executive officer of Albuquerque Therapy Services, Inc. She has worked for various organizations as an occupational therapist and in related fields since 1970. Ms. Windeck has been involved in exploring the relationships between sensory integration, speech and language, and learning, and has developed techniques for using the interrelationships among the three in therapy. She has developed many occupational therapy programs, including programs for home health and rehabilitation agencies, schools, and other public agencies, and programs for children with sensory integrative disorders.

Ms. Windeck received her B.S. from the University of Iowa in 1967 and her M.S. in learning disabilities from Marquette University in 1982.

Contents

Preface

This book was written by a parent and teacher for other parents and teachers. I hope you will find the information interesting as well as useful. There have been many pieces missing in my knowledge of how children learn and why they behave in particular ways. Learning about sensory integration has helped me to fill in many of these pieces and fit others more accurately into place. It is my hope that the information in this book will help you to fit the pieces into place and make life at home or in the classroom run a little more smoothly.

—Maryann Colby Trott, M.A.

Introduction:
What Is Sensory Integration?

You have probably discovered, often without conscious thought, the things that help you to relax, concentrate, or just feel good in various situations. You probably use many different techniques, depending on the requirements of different circumstances. Perhaps music helps you to concentrate when working but is distracting during conversations. Sometimes rough-and-tumble play with the kids makes you come alive. Other times you may not want to be in contact with anyone. A cup of coffee before work might be perfect, but at night a warm cup of cocoa is much more appealing. We often develop preferences because certain types of sensory input (activities, sounds, textures, and even foods) have helped us to respond appropriately in a given situation.

Our brains must be able to organize and process this sensory input, and to use that input to respond appropriately to a particular situation. To do so, we must integrate information we receive through all of our senses and from movement and gravity. It is easy to imagine how difficult life is for those who cannot hear or see adequately. It is more difficult to imagine what it must be like for those who are unable to understand what they hear and see. It is more difficult still to imagine what it is like for those who cannot understand the input they get from their tactile (sense of touch) and vestibular (movement and gravity) systems. The ability to learn even the simplest things and to behave appropriately in different situations, however, depends on these abilities.

Children, even very young children, must be able to take in information through all channels and perform many skills automatically. They must know and be comfortable with where their bodies are in relation to their environment; they must feel safe and know where and how they are being touched. They must also know, without being taught or told, what information to pay attention to and what to ignore.

Many children, however, don't know how to cope with the different sensory input they receive. They have difficulty organizing information and performing the many complex tasks necessary for learning and functioning in the world and, as Ayres has noted, "When the flow of sensation is disorganized, life can be like a rush-hour traffic jam" (1979). Children who, unlike the majority of their peers, are unable to process and use the sensory input they receive often have a sensory integrative disorder. A common component of this type of disorder is sensory defensiveness, in which children are unable to tolerate various kinds of sensory stimulation (Wilbarger and Wilbarger 1991). A sensory integrative disorder may, however, exist without sensory defensiveness.

It is not always easy to live with and love children. It is sometimes less easy to live with and love children who have a sensory integrative disorder. Sensory defensiveness can cause children to seek to control every aspect of their lives by being excessively demanding; unreasonably, explosively angry; picky; and bossy. But these children need all the help and support we can give them in order to prevent their lives from becoming so frustrating and unpleasant that they give up trying to learn and to please us and themselves. It is very easy to give them the impression that they can do nothing right and very difficult to let them know how much we love them and how very special and important they are. As Wilbarger and Wilbarger note, "treatment begins with understanding" (1991).

In the next few pages you will find a very brief, simple discussion of the tactile and vestibular systems as well as a discussion concerning praxis and arousal. If you are interested in learning more, refer to the bibliography. Chapter 6 includes information concerning how a sensory integrative disorder affects your child's life as well as your own, information about therapy and school, and some suggestions for meeting the challenges ahead. You may want to share this information with other family members and friends as well as teachers. Appendix B contains suggestions for teachers. If your child receives therapy, your child's therapist can provide you with more specific information.

A teacher's awareness of individual needs can make a difference in school performance and success.

Chapter 1

The Tactile and Vestibular Systems

The Tactile System

The tactile system is our sense of touch. It is through the tactile system that we first receive information about the world. Processing this information effectively allows us to feel safe, which in turn allows us to bond with those who love us and to develop socially and emotionally.

The tactile system is composed of two systems, the discriminative and the protective. The discriminative system allows us to determine where we are being touched and what it is that is touching us. Accurate discrimination requires us to register sensory input without sensory defensiveness. The protective system tells us when we are in contact with something dangerous and it causes a flight, fright, or fight response, which involves the whole mind and body. These responses happen in a hierarchy. When we first feel stress due to danger, we attempt to get away. If the stress continues, we may begin to exhibit signs of fear, such as increased respiration and heart rate, flushing, going pale, or losing our ability to move. Children may whine, cry, or become overly clingy. Finally, if we are still stressed, we fight. Discriminative and protective systems are extremely important for interpretation of information as well as for survival. In order for the tactile system to function efficiently, the discriminative and protective systems must perceive information correctly and work in balance.

Bonding through the tactile system is essential for early learning and social/emotional development.

Children whose tactile system is dysfunctional are likely to have a difficult time learning fine motor skills because it is through the discriminative system that the brain receives the feedback necessary to develop feeding, dressing, writing, and other fine motor skills. In addition, children with this dysfunction may have problems articulating sounds because they do not receive adequate information from the touch receptors in and around the face and mouth. Development of accurate visual perception and basic concepts also requires accurate discriminative information. Babies first see things in two dimensions. It is through tactile exploration (feeling objects with their hands, mouths, and any other available body parts)

The lifelong drive to receive tactile input is strongest in early childhood.

that they begin to understand the three-dimensional aspect of objects. Think about a baby who sees a ball. What the baby sees is a circle. Mom or Dad says "ball" and gives it to the baby. If the baby is receiving accurate information from the touch receptors and if the nervous system is correctly interpreting that information, holding and exploring the ball will help the baby begin to develop a concept of a sphere as opposed to a circle. It is almost impossible to imagine the number of early concepts that are developed in this way.

Poor tactile processing can lead to difficulty in learning letter formation.

Dysfunction in the tactile system may also cause the protective system to interpret ordinary contact as threatening. Imagine walking alone down an unknown, dark alley and suddenly feeling a hand on your arm. Your brain and body would immediately react! Children whose tactile systems give inaccurate information are frequently in this state of "red alert." Casual contact causes extreme reactions that may be interpreted as bad behavior. Children may react by running away (flight), whining and clinging (fright), or fighting with others. These behaviors may be physical or verbal.

Children who react with a flight response typically demonstrate a great deal of verbal and nonverbal avoidance behavior. They may attempt to move away from groups and make it quite clear, through their body language, that they do not want to be approached. Sometimes children will become class or family clowns, using jokes and mishaps to shift attention away from the situation that does not feel comfortable or safe. In school, they may be quite restless, constantly changing positions, frequently asking to go to the bathroom or to get a drink of water. Children may also use language to divert attention from themselves or the undesirable activity or task: "Yesterday, my mom said . . . " or "Yeah, but first I gotta . . . "

Tactile defensiveness is frequently a component of sensory defensiveness. Flight, fright, fight behaviors can result from combinations of sensory input.

Children who react to touch with a fright response may appear to be shy and reluctant to communicate. In some cases, the fright response may adversely affect early bonding with caregivers; in these cases, the lack of bonding is not related to whether parents are doing the "right" things for their babies. Inadequate bonding can influence early social and cognitive development as well as later language development necessary for interaction and communication. It may be difficult for children with this disorder to focus on and attend to others because so much of their attention is focused on the feeling of being in danger. Verbal communication often contains many phrases and sentences that are used to describe or manage the potential danger the children perceive. They may say "I can't" or "I'm not going to get hurt" in response to requests to perform certain tasks or participate in activities that they are quite able to perform.

Children who react with a fight response are often labeled "problems," since when they are confronted with an uncomfortable situation, they frequently use negative or resistive behavior and language, and they are physically or verbally aggressive. They can become quite agitated when people get close to them in certain ways but may get inappropriately close to others. These children may also have experienced difficulty in bonding with caregivers as infants. They may continue to have a hard time establishing the social interactions that are essential for developing communication. Their first words may include "messy," "stuck," or others that describe difficult or unpleasant situations. Later on, they may refuse to comply, call names, or make insulting remarks. It is very difficult for parents to hear and not feel hurt by remarks like "You're so stupid" or "I'll never do it." It is, however, important to respond in a way that helps children to know that we do understand their feelings of fear and discomfort and that we will help them to learn more appropriate ways of expressing themselves.

People with tactile defensiveness react strongly to tactile sensations. The condition may result from a combination of sensory input—for instance, when the noise of a crowded shopping mall causes the person to become tactilely defensive. Tactile defensiveness causes children to be very picky about clothing, sheets, and towels. They may dislike certain foods, not because of their flavors, but because of their textures. They are often resistant to getting their hands dirty or touching unfamiliar substances. They may be reluctant to be touched, especially by unfamiliar people, including relatives. What is intended to be a loving hug or a playful pat may be extremely unpleasant to children who have tactile defensiveness.

Children who are tactilely defensive may be said to feel too much. Some children, however, feel too little. Their brains don't register touch effectively, causing them to be slow or unable to determine when or where they are being touched. Some children do not register touch for a long time, but when they do, they react defensively. Other children may seem to have a high tolerance for pain simply because they do not accurately feel what is happening to them. They may not react to being too cold or too hot because they are unaware of the temperature. In infancy, such lack of registration inhibits babies' visual abilities to direct what their hands are doing. These abilities eventually enable children to look at one thing and work on something else with their hands at the same time. In school, for example, children must be able to write while looking at the board or a book. Individuals who cannot do this are limited in many areas.

Our brains require a certain amount of tactile information. This requirement varies from time to time and in various situations. If we do not get enough tactile input, or satiate our brains, we will react with touch "hunger." Children who do not register tactile information are always "hungry." They may be touching someone or something constantly, even when touching is inappropriate. They may also be unaware of the intensity of their touch and unable to judge how much pressure or force to apply.

Regardless of how tactile system dysfunction manifests itself, children with the condition need to be touched and have different kinds of tactile experiences, but these experiences must be carefully directed in order to help correct the erroneous messages received by the brain. If your child receives therapy for a tactile system dysfunction, a therapist can discuss with you, in greater depth, the specific elements of your child's problems.

The Vestibular System

Just as the tactile system is our sense of touch through which we develop relationships with others, the vestibular system is our sense of movement and gravity. It is through the vestibular system that we develop a relationship with the earth, that is, knowing what is right side up, upside down, left, right, horizontal, and vertical. The information we receive and process from this system is so basic to everything we do that it is very difficult to imagine what it would be like not to use that information correctly. The discussion provided here is, by necessity, quite short; it is a very simple discussion of a very complex issue.

Ayres notes, "The vestibular system is the unifying system. All other types of sensation are processed in reference to this basic vestibular information. The activity in the vestibular system provides a framework for the other aspects of our experiences" (1979). Thus input from the vestibular system paces the functioning of the entire central nervous system and prepares it for other sensory input.

Vestibular input tells us whether or not we are moving, how quickly we are moving, and in what direction we are moving. It provides us with that sense of safety that can come only from knowing that one's feet are planted firmly on the ground. It also gives us a physical reference that helps us make sense of visual information, particularly where we and other things in our environment are in relation to each other.

One of the earliest and ongoing tasks of infancy is developing body control to work against gravity.

Adequate muscle tone and posture allow us to move efficiently and to assume and maintain various positions comfortably throughout the day. One example of efficiency of movement is the ability to follow objects with our eyes. This ability is the foundation for the acquisition of basic academic skills such as reading and writing. The ability to move different body parts in unison is another important skill. Handwriting, for example, requires adequate control, stability, and rotation in the trunk and shoulder girdle.

Children have a strong drive to challenge their ability to work against gravity.

Another important skill related to the vestibular system is bilateral coordination, or the ability to use both sides of the body. This ability allows us to ride a bike, skip, jump rope, or play the piano. Bilateral coordination may be inhibited if hand dominance is not properly established. Children who do not process vestibular information efficiently may establish hand dominance so completely that they ignore the nondominant side of the body, or they may not establish adequate hand dominance. Either deficiency makes the performance of many common tasks quite difficult.

Children with vestibular system dysfunctions are likely to have problems with many of the components of daily living. They often appear to be uncoordinated and unable to perform skills requiring sequencing and timing. They are not always able to perceive visual information correctly. They may have poor memories and be slow to learn many basic academic skills. They may suffer from motion sickness no matter how short the journey or gentle the movement, or they may be very slow to get dizzy no matter how violent the movement. They are often reluctant to take part in physical activities or experiences that require them to move or use their bodies in a smooth, coordinated way.

Tactile and visual input are processed in relation to vestibular input.

A combination of many skills is required for bilateral control.

Trouble with memory and with learning basic academic skills is due in part to problems with processing auditory input. While we all need to move to some degree to listen (you may wiggle your leg or shift in your chair), children with vestibular system disorders need to move even more to listen and understand. Adults may be distracted by the amount of movement these children need. It is, however, important that we try not to tell children to "sit still and pay attention" when their brains are telling them to "get moving" so that they can attend and understand.

Research indicates that vestibular processes in the lower (subcortical) levels of the brain support processes that occur in higher (cortical) levels of the brain, including speech and language (Stilwell, Crowe, and McCallum 1978). Negative experiences with movement caused by a vestibular system dysfunction may, therefore, cause children to have trouble with speech and language, which are so essential for learning and social relationships. Language may not develop at the expected rate or it may not follow expected patterns of development; children may have difficulty using words to reflect what they know. They may also have difficulty later when they try to communicate with words and sentences.

Children with inadequate postural control expend enormous amounts of energy in tasks that ought to come automatically.

The goal of therapy is to provide positive experiences with movement that allow children to develop an organized way of looking at the world. These activities help them to move more efficiently and also to organize and use language to understand and describe their world and experiences.

Another aspect of communication that can be affected by vestibular system disorders is the ability to use nonverbal communication, or body language, appropriately. We communicate a great deal about our thoughts and feelings through the appropriate use of our faces and bodies. When people say one thing and nonverbally express another, the listener believes the nonverbal communication, regardless of the true intent. For example, if you tell friends that you love their vacation slides but yawn frequently and check the time as you watch, they believe you are bored to tears.

Communicating in this way requires adequate muscle tone. The speaker must also be able to coordinate the muscle activity with the language used. The vestibular system is very important in developing and modulating these components.

Children with a dysfunction in this area may be frequently misunderstood without knowing why, which can be very frustrating for them and for the people around them. The children may react inappropriately to such misunderstandings.

A dull or flat expression caused by low muscle tone may result in inaccurate social feedback.

Children with inaccurate vestibular processing may have inappropriate emotional reactions and behaviors in much the same way that those with inaccurate tactile processing may. Children who are unsure about the possible danger of falling or where they are in relation to the other people and objects in their environment will have a hard time behaving appropriately. They may actually be uncertain whether or not they are moving and are frequently afraid of falling. Walking on gravel, textured cement, or a metal grating may be quite threatening. This gravitational insecurity causes children to use their vision to monitor each situation and prevents them from moving with confidence and ease. This in turn inhibits their ability to observe and learn in various situations. It is not always possible to reassure them since what their brains are telling them takes precedence over what we are telling them. Other children do not experience gravitational insecurity, but their "hunger" for vestibular input causes them constantly to seek new and/or more intensive movement experiences. These children seem to have no fear at all and will take unreasonable risks in their quest to satisfy their hunger for vestibular input. In both cases, we must help children to stay safe and let them know that we understand their feelings and needs while helping them to find safe ways of dealing with their difficulties.

Fear may inhibit a child's drive to explore the world through movement.

Chapter 2

Products of Sensory Processes

Praxis

Praxis is what allows us to organize, plan, and execute skills of all kinds in a refined and efficient manner. Praxis is observable beginning at around seven or eight months. Some of it occurs involuntarily, some of it occurs automatically and unconsciously, and some of it requires our highest level of cognitive thought. It is sometimes incorrectly assumed that children who develop common skills such as rolling over, sitting up, vocalizing, crawling, walking, and so forth, at the appropriate ages have adequate praxis. The early developmental milestones, however, do not require praxis. They are centrally programmed into children's brains and tend to occur in nearly the same sequence and during the same general time period for most children. The acquisition of these skills at appropriate ages indicates that the brain and motor system are basically intact. It does not indicate whether or not children are able to process, organize, and integrate information about the world. This ability is critical to sensory integrative development.

There are several components of praxis and all require accurate information from the tactile, vestibular, proprioceptive (the information we receive from muscles, tendons, and joints that allows us to know where our body parts are at any given moment), auditory, and visual systems. In this section, we will provide a simple overview of the components of praxis. These components are imitation, ideation, initiation, construction, feedback, feed-forward, grading, timing, sequencing, and motor planning.

Imitation is an aspect of praxis that can be observed early in life. Many early parent-baby games involve imitation. Parents imitate babies' movements, facial expressions, or vocalizations. Babies then repeat the action that the parents imitated. These first conversations are very important to the development of praxis and also vital to bonding between parents and infants. This infant ability to organize facial expression and body language leads to the later ability to use gesture, facial expression, and so forth. Throughout life, we most clearly communicate what we are feeling through nonverbal means. When babies are not able to process input and organize responses, sensory-motor development is delayed and social-emotional development is often affected.

Imitation forms the basis for developing later motor skills and communicative ability.

Another developmental aspect of praxis is ideation. Ideation begins when children are able to base their interactions not only on imitation of others, but also on ideas they have generated and can communicate. Children will usually experiment to see how different things move and how they can move their bodies in relation to those things. They are constantly crawling over or under, swinging, walking, running, or jumping on whatever happens to be available. In order to do these things children must see the possibilities in the environment and organize their motor responses. Children who have problems with praxis do not see their environment in terms of movement possibilities. They often interact in only one way and that one interaction does not improve over time. They may appear to be purposeless, running around or standing in a space rather than exploring the features of that space and challenging their bodies to perform in new ways. Some children are able to imitate but may not be able to generate ideas of their own. While imitating other children during activities they may become confused if the activity changes; they often get stuck with the name "copy-cat."

Ideation allows for constant revision of ideas and actions.

As with many of the aspects of praxis, ideation has a language component. Difficulty with ideation may manifest itself in problems with communicating new ideas. From a relatively early age, children should be able to use communication to respond or answer, to describe or comment, to label, to request or direct, to get attention, and to protest or deny (Laurel and Elledge 1985). Children who are unable to generate or communicate new ideas often use only one or two of these types of communication. These children are frequently more likely to relate to adults than to other children since children are less able to understand communication limitations.

The ability to think of new things is also essential in academic work.

Children must also be able to initiate activities. In order to do this, they must have a clear idea of how to begin a certain activity. What appears to be quite simple to us, as adults, may be overwhelmingly complex to children. Many times, children who have trouble with praxis give up on a task before they begin, simply because it appears so complex that they don't have a clue as to how to begin and may not be able to use language to help them figure it out.

Lack of organization can compound learning problems.

Construction is another aspect of developmental praxis. It allows us to put objects together in new and different ways. Children use constructional praxis when they create objects with blocks. This kind of praxis also allows them to organize a play area for different purposes and, therefore, makes an important contribution to the development of language. The

The developmental drive to explore construction may contribute to the persistent popularity of construction toys.

ability to build a store or school or have a tea party with the objects available in a room is a precursor to the ability to use abstract thought. Constructional praxis is also important in learning how to organize work spaces, drawers, closets, desks, or lockers. Experienced teachers can often predict which children are likely to have difficulty with certain learning tasks by looking at how those children organize their desks and how well they are able to organize themselves for work. Children who consistently forget to bring books, papers, pencils, and other materials to class may have deficits in constructional praxis.

Feedback is the information we get from proprioception that allows us to refine motor skills. As we repeat tasks, our performance becomes automatic and we know what the correct patterns feel like. If what we are doing doesn't feel right, we change our performance slightly until it does feel right. Feedback creates a memory of how things are done. That memory can be used again and again in the same or similar situations and can also be changed slightly to fit new situations. Children who do not have adequate feedback may work very hard to learn a new motor act or concept and be unable to remember that information in the next week, day, or even ten minutes.

Feed-forward is the component of praxis that allows us unconsciously to anticipate the next step, strength, or speed required to perform a certain motor act. We have all had the experience of preparing to pick up a heavy suitcase and using too much force for the actual weight; in such instances our feed-forward ability is tricked by appearances.

Feedback and feed-forward work together to help us perform tasks efficiently. Without any conscious awareness, our brains compare what was anticipated to happen (feed-forward) to what actually did happen (feedback). This comparison allows us to self-correct an error quickly. The ability to write or type quickly and

Coloring in the lines requires both feedback and feed-forward.

efficiently is an example. When you are writing or typing, you know what the next letter should feel like and your fingers quickly and unconsciously move into the correct pattern. When you make an error, feedback and feed-forward cause you to feel the error before you see it.

Our ability to grade motor acts is what allows us to vary the intensity of what we do. Grading allows us to catch balls of different sizes, climb stairs of various heights, and turn the steering wheel of the car just the right amount. Almost everything we do requires some degree of grading. You would use a different intensity of movement to pat a baby to sleep than you would to congratulate a quarterback. Children who have deficits in praxis are unable to make these judgments and may unintentionally hurt their peers. They may gain reputations as bullies simply because they are unable to be gentle.

Timing and sequencing allow us to perform motor acts at the appropriate time and in the correct order. In addition, they help us to string movements together without hesitating or stopping. Timing and sequencing require an ability to perceive correctly and understand visual space, speed, and distance, and to understand how we move in relation to an environment that may or may not be in motion. This ability, in turn, requires accurate information from the vestibular system as well as the ability to follow objects with both eyes. Our ability to sequence is also somewhat dependent on our ability to use language to talk our way through the completion of a task. We are sometimes aware of this process, particularly when we perform a new or difficult task. It is, however, more common that we do it without even being aware of using language to sequence tasks. If you are playing catch and make all the right moves at all the wrong times, the game is not going to be very successful. If you learn all that is required to drive a car but perform the skills in the wrong sequence, you are not likely to pass the driver's test. If you had to stop every few seconds to figure out the next move, how efficiently could you write?

Knowing how hard to squeeze the glue bottle requires adequate grading.

Motor planning is what allows us to create, use, and combine various motor skills to perform new, more complex acts. After a new act has been planned and used several times (that is, practiced), it becomes automatic. Even seemingly simple tasks, such as feeding, dressing, and getting from one place to another require motor planning until the skill becomes automatic. Other tasks, such as speaking, writing, riding a bike, or jumping rope are exceedingly complex and require a great deal of motor planning when they are first attempted or, in some cases, whenever a component of the act is new or slightly different.

Perhaps the best way of illustrating the roles of the different aspects of praxis is through an example. Most of us can relate to the experience of learning how to drive a car. Initially, we had to think about the placement of our hands, legs, and feet (imitation, motor planning, feedback, and feed-forward). We had to think about how much pressure to apply and how far to turn the wheel to head in the desired direction. We were probably unable to do anything in a smooth, efficient manner

Sports require a fine sense of timing and sequencing.

(feedback, feed-forward, grading, timing, sequencing, and motor planning). Most of us had to talk our way through each step, using our language skills to help us figure out how to perform each step (sequencing and motor planning). Eventually, the skill became automatic and we no longer have to think about how to drive a car each time we want to go somewhere. Our legs and arms make the proper responses smoothly and efficiently without our conscious thought.

Motor planning allows for development of age appropriate pretend play.

Many children with sensory processing problems have difficulty with one or more of the components of praxis. Frequently, they have difficulty creating, organizing, or learning new movement patterns or combining those patterns into new sequences. These children appear to be clumsy and accident prone. They may trip and fall over nothing or over their own feet, and may seem to be constantly running into things. They may also frequently drop things because they are unable to plan adequately or grade the motor patterns required to pick up and carry them. Simple rhythm or other activities, such as jumping rope or catching a ball, require timing and sequencing and may be quite difficult. Even practicing a certain skill a great deal will not always help. Children may not be able to learn how it feels to do some things efficiently. This is referred to as an inability to process feedback and can change from day to day so that children who are able to perform a certain skill one day may not be able to do it the next day, no matter how hard they try.

Feedback, feed-forward, grading, timing, sequencing and motor planning are all components of praxis that are required to do a familiar activity in an unfamiliar setting.

The ability to use language to plan and organize before an activity is a very important part of praxis. Very young children begin pairing movement and words early in their development (Meacham 1979). You may hear young children talking to themselves as they perform certain motor tasks such as going down a slide. At this point their movement and words are not necessarily related to each other. Later, children will use words to describe the outcome of their movement, such as saying "slide down," after getting to the bottom of the slide. Eventually, children begin to use language to describe their goals and compare these goals to the outcome of the activity. On the slide, you may hear something like "I'm gonna slide down backwards, then turn around . . . oops!—I didn't turn around." Just as children may have difficulty using language because of problems processing information that comes from movement and touch, they may also have difficulty continuing to develop praxis because of problems using language for organization. Children who are unable to use language in this way may have a difficult time "talking themselves through" new or difficult activities.

All of us experience some difficulty in these areas from time to time and, obviously, some of us are better than others in certain skills. We learn to avoid or compensate for the things that we cannot do well. It is, however, important to experience more success than failure and to perform basic skills without having to think about how to do them. For some children the goal of therapy is to improve sensory processing which will, in addition to other strategies, improve praxis. Improved praxis will help to clear the "roadblocks" in the brain and allow children to be better able to perform old skills and learn new skills with confidence and ease.

Alertness

In order to behave appropriately in various situations, to learn, and to develop language, we must be able to take in information of all kinds (visual, auditory, tactile, vestibular) and correctly process that information without overloading or shutting down. If you are overstimulated by the noise, flashing lights, and fast movement on a carnival ride, for example, you probably won't be able to understand much of what someone is saying, express yourself very well, or behave in your usual manner. On the other hand, if you are trying to attend to a lecture after lunch in a hot, dark room with little stimulation, you are unlikely to understand the concepts presented in the lecture and you may appear to be very bored, even though you actually find the subject matter quite interesting. Our ability to attend, learn, and behave appropriately is dependent, in part, on our state of arousal or alertness.

What looks like boredom or inattention may actually be low alertness.

Our state of arousal probably changes several times during the day. For most of us it is fairly low as we awake and then rises as we get up and move about. During the rest of the day we automatically do various things that help us to stay alert. It is in this alert state that we are best able to attend and learn. If, for various reasons, our state of arousal drops too low or rises too high, we must be able to regain the alert state that lies between the high and low states. We use movement of various kinds to regain this state. If you are feeling particularly lazy in the afternoon after lunch, you may take a quick walk around the block and feel much better. If, on the other hand, you are very angry about something that has just happened, that walk will help to calm you down.

Inconsistent work performance may be the result of varying states of alertness.

Getting along with others is difficult when alertness is too high or too low.

A normal state of arousal develops as a result of the ability to regulate or modulate sensory input. Children with sensory integrative disorders are often unable to maintain an appropriate state of alertness through ordinary activities. Children who are commonly in a state of low arousal may require a great deal of proprioceptive input (heavy work of the large muscles and joints) to bring up their state of arousal. Ordinary sensory stimulation causes some other children to be in an almost constant state of high arousal. These children require similar proprioceptive input to achieve a lower, more normal, state of arousal.

If their state of arousal is too low, children look as though they are tired or bored. They may appear to be "lazy" and difficult to please. They are often reluctant to participate in activities and may spend more time in sedate pastimes, such as watching television or reading, than they do at active play. They can also become quite upset over minor occurrences or ordinary requests. Their reaction may be similar to one we may have if we are very tired or not feeling well.

When arousal is too high a fright, flight or fight response may occur.

If their state of arousal is too high, children cannot be still long enough to complete tasks. They seem to be constantly in motion yet unable to engage in purposeful activities, even those requiring a great deal of movement. Their emotions are constantly on edge and they frequently blow up.

A normal state of arousal is essential for impulse control. In some situations, we may be able to sit, attend, and accomplish the tasks before us because our nervous system inhibits impulses that tell us inaccurately that we are not safe. In other situations, our language helps us to control impulses. When you see an expensive item that you might really like to have, your first impulse may be "I'm going to buy it!" It is usually not very long, however, before you begin to use your language to control that impulse. "Can I really afford it? Do I really need it? What will I do with it? I better forget it!"

It is not uncommon to hear teachers complain that certain students have no impulse control. Quite frequently, those students are the ones who are not usually in an optimal state of arousal. The unconscious impulses telling them that they are not safe are not under control since the brain is not receiving or interpreting information correctly. In addition, children in a high or low state of arousal are not able to use their language to help them control other impulses. Inability to use language in this way is one reason some children are frequently in trouble even though they "know better."

As adults, most of us have discovered the things that help us to achieve and maintain an appropriate state of arousal. For the most part, we have chosen careers, hobbies, and leisure activities that fit our needs. We also usually have the freedom to move around, change tasks, sip drinks, chew gum, have a snack, or use other means to help us stay alert and attend. Children, however, do not always know what they need and do not always have the same freedoms that we take for granted.

The sensory requirements of sitting in a group can affect state of arousal.

We may also make demands that are difficult for children to meet. Sitting quietly during mealtimes, church services, or adult conversations is difficult for all children at times. It may even be difficult for some children to attend to stories, games, or other appropriate children's entertainments. It is more difficult for children who are not adequately processing the sensory information they are receiving and are not, therefore, able to maintain an appropriate state of arousal.

Movement of various kinds is the key to helping children maintain optimal states of arousal and is easy to build into daily routines. There are several suggestions in chapter 6 that may be helpful.

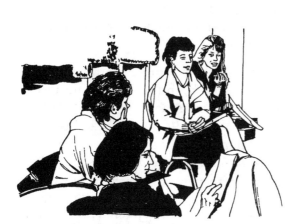

The next time you meet with a group of adults, note the variety of activities used to maintain alertness.

The atmosphere of common family activities can be affected by state of alertness.

Chapter 3

What Helps Us to Process Sensory Information?

We all have different ways of arriving at and maintaining a state of alertness that allows us to work, play, learn, rest, and perform in all areas of our lives. Many of the habits and preferences that we develop are a result of our efforts to meet our sensory needs. This chapter is intended to help you determine the kinds of things you use to help process the information you receive throughout the day, which in turn may help you to understand your children's needs. Keep in mind that we have different requirements for falling and staying asleep, waking up, working, playing, learning, or just "hanging out."

In each list below, use one color to circle those things that you like. Use another color to circle those things that you do not like. You may want to add other preferences (positive or negative) specific to your own tastes. In addition, think about specific times when you like to use certain things. For example, rocking may relax you before bedtime but may inhibit your concentration while you are working. You may want to make notes in the margins.

Food and Oral Activity

Oral input provides a subtle way to help us maintain focused attention.

Sweet Foods

ice cream or milk shakes

cookies

soda (with caffeine or without?)

gum (how much?)

soft candy

puddings or creamy desserts

dried fruits (what kind?)

sweet rolls

jelly

chocolate

cake

hard candy

candy bars

(what kind?)

At this point, you may see a pattern emerging. Do most of the sweet things that you chose have similar textures? Do you prefer combinations of textures such as cake with nuts or ice cream on a cone? Which things do you suck on or drink with a straw? Which do you lick? Which do you crunch on? Which are chewy foods?

(This chapter is based on a more comprehensive work by Patti Oetter; in press.)

Salty or Crunchy Foods

crackers	nuts
popcorn	chips (potato or tortilla?)
pretzels	bagels or breadsticks
jerky	cheese
peanut butter	raw vegetables
ice (do you suck or crunch?)	cereal

How do you eat these foods? Do you like to dip some of them into other foods such as soft cheeses or salad dressings? If so, which foods do you dip and what do you dip them into? Which are crunchy foods? Which are chewy foods?

Sour Foods

lemons (lemonade)	grapefruit (grapefruit juice)
candy sour balls	unsweetened yogurt
cranberry juice	

Fruit/Fruit Juices

apples	prunes	bananas
pineapple	grapes	peaches
strawberries	oranges	melons
plums	apricots	nectarines
cherries		

Spicy Foods

salt	pepper	mustard
ketchup	salad dressings	pizza
spaghetti	chili	cinnamon
salsa	horseradish	tartar sauce

The foods and food textures that you indicated as preferences are those foods and food textures that can help you to process and organize information. Over the next several days you may want to make note of the foods that you choose in various situations. What do you choose as a snack (or do with your mouth) when you are in the middle of a complex project? What do you choose for a bedtime snack? What do you like in the morning to help you wake up? What helps you to attend to a lecture or discussion? It may be helpful to discuss these issues with the important people in your life. Others are often more aware of our preferences than we may be ourselves. You may want to add some neglected items to your grocery list.

It is common to see children use their tongues when their hands are engaged in a difficult task.

The next time you thumb through a sports magazine, focus on pictures of athletes who are performing feats that are physically challenging. Notice the peculiar positions of their tongues or the strange shape of their mouths. You may observe the same thing anytime you see someone performing a difficult task. Actions like these help all of us to process information and organize the complex motor patterns involved in performing complicated tasks. We may put our hands to our mouths or use toothpicks at frequent intervals. Some of us chew on gum, pencils, fingernails, hair, or a mustache. Perhaps we run our tongues across our teeth or chew on our tongues, cheeks, or lips. Many of us like to sip drinks throughout the day. Others may smoke to fill the need for oral stimulation.

Tactile Activity

We also have very distinct preferences concerning joint and muscle activity, touch, and temperature. In each of the following sections, indicate which things you do or like to do and which things you do not do or like to do.

Joint and Muscle Activity

clenching teeth
pushing hands together
pushing/pulling
carrying
wrestling
hiking (not walking)
playing football
rowing
pushing out or pulling on
  chairs while seated

biting pencils (pens, and so forth)
popping fingers or other joints
lifting
hanging by your arms
lifting weights
climbing
biking
stretching

Joint and muscle activity provides input from within the body (proprioception).

Deep Pressure

heavy massage
being underwater
bear hugs
being wrapped in blankets
heavy quilts on beds

Forms of deep pressure that appeal to some people may cause fear reactions in others.

Touch Pressure

> back rubs
> applying lotion
> being stroked

Light Touch

> back scratches
> light tickles
> feeling hair or fur
> light scratching or brushing on the face or
>   around the mouth

We all have very definite preferences concerning tactile input. The kinds of clothing, bedding, and furniture we choose, the way we wear our hair, and what we do with our hands when we are idle or for relaxation are, in part, related to our tactile preferences. Our mates and others who know us well can probably identify the kinds of input that please us.

Touch pressure experiences throughout childhood are an important part of parent/child interactions and continue to assist us in forming close relationships throughout life.

Our close relationships are, in part, based on giving and receiving tactile input. We often hear that people who live alone are happier and healthier when they have pets. This may be related to the tactile input provided by contact with an animal.

Light touch often carries a strong emotional component. The amount of light touch desirable or tolerable can be highly variable even within the same person.

Children vary in the amount of clothing needed or comfortable for them.

Temperature

Our temperature preferences are related to our tactile preferences. Having extreme preferences about temperature or difficulties with temperature regulation may be indicative of processing problems. Individuals who are having a flight, fright, or fight reaction may feel clammy. These people may also feel overheated in such circumstances. Being hot and sweaty causes many of us to become tactilely defensive to a certain extent, since contact may be uncomfortable. While answering the questions below, ask yourself if your answers may be different under differing circumstances.

Compared to others:
- Do you tend to over- or underdress for the weather?
- What temperature do you prefer in the bath or shower?
- What temperature do you prefer the water to be when you do dishes?
- At what temperature do you prefer your food?
- Do you turn red easily?
- Do you sweat without much exertion?
- Do you become overheated easily during sleep or activities?

The choices that you made above should give you some idea of the temperature at which you function most effectively.

Movement

This section has to do with the ways we use movement to relax and to achieve and maintain alertness and a sense of physical competence that results from moving our bodies against gravity. In the sections below, indicate your preferences. Some selections relate to types and intensity of movement and others relate to ways in which we are able to enjoy challenging gravity. Some activities require little or no time commitment and can be used throughout the day; others require more time and are, therefore, used less frequently. Some activities may be incorporated into hobbies, exercise routines, or other common work, play, or relaxation activities.

Oscillation Activities

(bouncing, jumping, or moving your entire body, a part of your body, or an object up and down)

chewing or crunching
tapping pens, pencils, etc.
running in place
hopscotch
skipping steps while
  on stairs
sitting on foot and
  bouncing
aerobic dance or exercise
trampoline
gymnastics (bars)
track (hurdles, broad jump,
  pole vault, high jump)

tapping heel, toe,
  or foot
weight lifting
jumping rope
stretching arms
  and shoulders
jumping jacks
teeter totter
bouncing on balls
bouncing on beds
gymnastics (vault)
gymnastics
  (floor exercise)

Oscillation provides an easy way to increase state of alertness.

Linear Activities

(moving in a line or back and forth)
    swinging a leg or foot
    swinging an object
    shaking out arms or hands
    swinging on doors or gates
    sitting in a chair on wheels or one with a moving back
    rocking in a rocking chair
    biking
    walking
    swinging
    skiing
    skateboarding
    roller or ice skating
    riding a scooter
    sliding

Many people crave linear movement. Children require it for the development of normal sensory processing.

Rotary Activities

(going around and around or partially around)
    twisting upper body
    twirling hair or other object
    twirling a baton
    playing statue maker
    twirling arms
    tumbling
    twirling around
    twisting a swing
    somersaulting
    rolling
    sitting and spinning
    pushing or riding a merry-go-round

- Do you enjoy carnival, fair, or amusement park rides that I have not mentioned? If so, which ones?
- Can you determine what kinds of movement are involved in the rides you enjoy?

Rotary input is most effective when done by the child rather than another person.

(Keep in mind your answers to these questions as you read through the next section.)

The kinds of movement that you indicated a preference for are kinds of movement that can be used to help you organize information. When you are feeling stressed try a few minutes of your favorite activities.

Gravity

Since gravity receptors are located in the ear, how comfortable we feel with our heads in various positions reflects our sense of competence against gravity. When we are "grounded" we feel comfortable and safe. We may, therefore, choose to support ourselves in various ways in order to concentrate or relax. Not having to work against gravity gives us more energy to think on the highest levels. This is one of the reasons we may hold our heads up with our hands when we are deep in thought. We may also hold the head up with one hand and write with the other. Many of us find it relaxing to lie on the couch or in a hammock and read the Sunday paper. In this position we do not have to work against gravity at all and can concentrate better.

Not having to work against gravity can help us to concentrate.

Many daily experiences involve interaction with unstable surfaces that challenge our sense of gravity. Some of them, such as walking from concrete to grass, walking on gravel, or moving up and down curbs, are done with little or no awareness. Others, such as going up or down a hill, walking on open-backed stairs, going on an escalator or moving walkway, are experiences we may seek or avoid. There are also times when we purposely challenge our competence against gravity by walking on a curb, climbing a tree or ladder, or carrying more items than we are comfortable with rather than making two trips.

Keeping in mind that gravity is challenged only when the head is not supported in any way, choose one of the following positions when you answer the questions below:

Head in vertical position—standing or sitting upright with head aligned with body.

Head in horizontal position—lying on stomach or back with head aligned with body (not supported).

Head in position out of straight planes—on the diagonal or some other position not in alignment with the rest of the body.

Head down or leaning backward.

- Which position do you choose in order to work or concentrate?
- Which position do you choose when you are reading for pleasure?
- Which position do you choose when you are reading more difficult or complex material?
- Which position do you use when you are writing?
- Which position do you choose when you are having a friendly conversation?
- Which position do you choose when you are studying?

We relate to gravity in many other ways in our daily lives. Can you think of ways in which you enjoy challenging gravity?

The positions you indicated are positions in which you are best able to concentrate, relax, and organize your thoughts. You may use alternative positions and movements on unstable surfaces (such as sitting on your foot or rocking back in your chair) in combination with your favorite subtle movements (hair twirling, pencil tapping, and so on) during activities that require you to sit in one place. Sitting in a completely supported position for a long time decreases our ability to attend. Many adults who have jobs that require them to sit for long periods of time choose chairs that roll, rock back, or allow them to sit in different, less stable, ways in order to maintain alertness.

We all choose various ways of supporting ourselves in order to concentrate, relax, and perform various tasks.

We have all formed "habits" that help us to concentrate. The people closest to us are likely to recognize the positions we commonly use for various tasks. Children and teenagers are notorious for the uncommon positions they choose for working, reading, and relaxing. They have, however, chosen these positions because their brains are best able to perform the necessary functions when their bodies are supported in these particular ways. You may want to reconsider insisting that children *sit* at their desks in order to study "properly."

Now, check back to your answers regarding rides in the movement section. Do the rides you enjoy involve challenging gravity as well as a particular kind of movement? Are there ways in which challenging gravity makes you uncomfortable?

Visual and Auditory Input

The sections on visual and auditory input are difficult to put into a questionnaire format because the ways in which we use visual and auditory information reflect how well our brains integrate information from the other sensory systems. We do, however, have preferences and personal strengths and weaknesses in the ways in which we use, or prefer to receive, auditory and visual information.

Visual Input

- Do you prefer direct or indirect lighting?
- Do you prefer natural or artificial light?
- How intense do you like light to be?
- What wattage bulb do you use?

Research indicates that some people suffer from seasonal depression that is related to the absence of intense light during certain times of the year. Do you suffer from this depression or do you think you might if you lived in a different area of the country?

We are visually attracted to objects in our environment early in life.

Light helps us to initiate and maintain alertness. The preferences you indicated should tell you what kind of light helps you most and where to place the light to be most beneficial. Keep in mind that we usually associate bright light with warm temperature. How do your answers concerning light relate to your answers concerning temperature in the section on tactile activities?

Color helps us to orient, attend, and learn. Children tend to prefer intense primary colors. It is not coincidental that many learning materials for children are full of bright red, yellow, and blue.

- What are your color preferences?
- Are the colors you choose for your bedroom different from those you would choose for your office?
- Do graphs or charts done in color help you to understand the material they are intended to illustrate?
- Do you use color coding to help you when making lists, studying, or prioritizing the things you must do?

We use visual information, as well as other kinds of sensory information, to alert and calm ourselves and to help us focus and attend. In addition, we depend on visual information to help us to define our own boundaries, to define our place or location in the environment, and to define the way we move through time and space. Each one of these ways in which we use visual information has three distinct components.

We are able to understand and respect the personal space of others because of our ability to integrate visual, tactile, and vestibular information. We all have distinct preferences for personal space. These preferences differ slightly from person to person and in various situations. We do not often think about this ability, but if you have ever been in a situation in which a person did not allow you enough personal space, you are certainly aware of how important it can be. People who are chronically unable to respect the property of others also have an inadequate sense of personal space.

Our need for boundaries in our environment changes as we grow. A very young child needs a large space in order to explore the environment. An adult can do with a much smaller environment, such as a desk. Think about the way elementary school classrooms are organized. The kindergarten classroom has no individual desks. Very young children are still learning how to deal with the demands of movement and gravity and are not ready to have their personal environment confined to a small space or cluttered by too many large objects. As the age of the children increases, however, the amount of personal environment they are allowed decreases. Older children are expected to be able to manage gravity and movement and should, therefore, do well with a smaller personal environment.

Our boundaries also change as we grow. People who have no concept of the safety of moving through various environments may have an inadequate perception of boundaries. Babies feel safest when they can see their caretakers. When they are first capable of independent movement, they will usually stay in the same room. An older baby (around nine months) will wander down the hall. A two-year-old will play alone in the yard. A-five-year-old will cross the street, and a nine-year-old is likely to ride a bike around the block. Adults feel safe exploring many miles away from home. As our abilities to deal with the demands of movement and gravity increase, we are more willing to move through larger areas of space.

Exploration of the environment is dependent on our ability to see the possibilities.

How we go about keeping ourselves organized in various ways relates to how we use visual information in our environment. We have all formed distinct ways of keeping track of our personal belongings. It is unlikely that two people would organize their clothing, toilet articles, or purse or pocket contents in the same way. Each of us also has distinct ways of organizing our working environments. Given duplicate sets of work materials and the space to contain them, we would each organize them in slightly different ways.

In order to accomplish the various tasks required of us we must constantly redefine our place in the environment. If you take a moment to give some conscious thought to what you usually do unconsciously, you will notice that you have a particular way and order in which you organize your home, dress yourself, write, follow directions, and accomplish a host of other tasks. The way in which you move your body parts through the environment in order to complete various tasks is, in part, dependent upon the way in which you use visual information to define your place in the environment.

We also use visual information to change our location in the environment. In order to do this, we must first be able to define our present location. For example, when you use a map you must first identify your current location. Only after you have determined where you are will you be able to determine in which direction you need to move in order to get where you want to be. We differ in our abilities to use this kind of information and in the kinds of visual information we use. Think about the landmarks you use to find the grocery store when you are driving or the ones you use to find your way home after a walk or bicycle ride. You also use landmarks, both visual and tactile, to find your bathroom or kitchen in the dark. If you move to a different place, you have to find new landmarks.

Obviously, it is essential that we use visual information in order to help us to move through space. This too, however, is an area in which our preferences and abilities vary. In order to move through space, we must catalog and retain information about our personal location (and that of our body parts), the location of objects and people in the environment, and the options for change. This cataloging activity can be illustrated through thinking about what is required in order to answer the telephone. The first thing to be considered is where your body parts are. If you are sitting on your foot or have your legs crossed, you must first move those body parts into appropriate positions. If you are seated at a table or desk or have items in your lap, you must figure out how to get around those things. Finally, you must determine where the phone is and how to get from your present location to that of the phone.

Although these are things we never really think about, we have all experienced occasional difficulty in accomplishing such simple tasks. This may be due to a temporary lapse in our ability to integrate sensory information. It is amazing that we are usually so efficient in this area that we are able to negotiate our way through a crowd of people whose locations are constantly changing. We can sometimes even do this with a load of packages or a plate full of food.

Once again, it is important to point out that efficient processing of vestibular information is strongly related to the ability to use visual information. It is the efficient integration of vestibular information that contributes to the understanding of spatial relationships. This understanding allows us to use left to right and top to bottom progression in such complex skills as reading and writing. Stability in the head and visual field, which is also dependent on accurate vestibular information, allows us to differentiate between the letters that differ only in terms of how one part of the letter relates to left/right and top/bottom. Examples are q, p, g, b, d, n, and u. Would you be able to distinguish between those letters, or read and write efficiently, if you were uncertain about how the letters and words were related to a given position in space?

So much of what we take for granted is really quite complex. Think about the issues discussed here as you go about ordinary tasks in the next few days. Can you imagine what it might be like to be less efficient in various ways? Can you identify your own strengths and weaknesses? Do certain colors, patterns, lightings, or their intensities affect your mood, alertness, or ability to concentrate? Do you have a hard time keeping track of objects? Can you use a map or the mall directory when you need to? Do you frequently bump into things if the furniture is rearranged? Does it take a long time for you to figure out how to negotiate a new building? When you are tired or distracted, do you lose track of where you are reading on a page or confuse common words?

Auditory Input

The final area we will consider is that of auditory information. Auditory information can be the most difficult for the brain to organize, integrate, understand, and use. Auditory input also has an impact (as does all sensory information) on our level of alertness.

The amount of auditory input that we like or are willing to tolerate is very definite. People with differing auditory tolerance levels who share the same living space are likely to have to find ways of compromising. There are probably many marriages that have been saved due to the introduction of earphones.

Vibration is both auditory (we hear it) and tactile (we feel it). The higher the frequency of the vibration, the higher the pitch. The same frequencies that are irritating to some of us may be pleasing or calming to others. As in all other areas, each of us has distinct preferences.

Which of the following sounds do you like, dislike, or not notice?

drums (bass, snare, etc.)	white noise
vacuum cleaner	blender
refrigerator	brushing your teeth
water pik	vibrator
fans	dryer/washer
phones	sirens
watches (wind-up, battery)	clocks (wind-up, electric, etc.)
ice maker	cold air return
disposal	car, bus, or truck engines
furnace	riding over metal or wood bridges
riding over cattle guards	riding over gravel or dirt roads
rustling and creaks in pillows, beds, and furniture	

For the following questions, think about the answers you might give if you were tired, ill, depressed, happy, working, playing, or relaxing.

- When listening to speech or music, do you prefer a steady or an unsteady rhythm?
- How loud do you like music or the TV? When?
- What style(s) of music do you like? When?
- What types of instruments do you like to listen to (woodwinds, brass, strings, percussion)? When?
- Do you prefer instrumental or vocal music? When?
- What type of vocal music do you prefer (opera, choral, etc.)? When?
- Do you listen to music or television when you are concentrating?
- Do you like to have the radio or television going almost all the time?

Do you now, or did you when you were younger, want to have music or TV on when you were studying or going to sleep? (The developmental requirements of children through puberty include intensity of input. That is one of the reasons why children are notorious for liking their music very loud with a heavy bass beat.)

Are there certain voice qualities (tone, pitch, rhythm, loudness) that are easier for you to listen to, understand, and learn from?

If so, what are they?

Language

- How well, and comfortably, do you explain things and express your thoughts and feelings?
- How easy is it for you to produce written language?
- How well do you understand other people's spoken language?
- How about written language?
- How well do you use facial expression, "body language," gestures, and signs? (You may want to ask someone else this question.)
- How well do you understand nonverbal language?

Exploration of the environment through movement, touch, and vision helps the child form the bases of language.

Although these questions are very difficult to answer, you probably have a good idea where your personal strengths and weaknesses lie. All language, verbal, nonverbal, and written, requires the most complex integration of sensory and motor information. It is an abstraction of personal experiences, and the ability to share and relate to experiences is essential in developing relationships with others.

Although language is the most common way to relate to others in social and learning situations it is also the most difficult because it is so personal. When we have problems in this area it may be helpful to seek the kind of input we need in order to help us to concentrate, attend, and understand what is being said or read. That input may be as simple as chewing on a pencil or jiggling a foot. It may have to be as intensive as taking a break to eat or get some exercise. There is a good reason why taking a walk while talking can help communication.

We hope you have found this section useful in helping to understand your own sensory needs as well as those of the people around you. Once again, please remember that this is a very simple discussion of a complex issue. You would need an intensive interview with a trained therapist to understand your sensory needs more thoroughly.

Learning to converse involves a complex understanding of another's verbal and nonverbal communication as well as the ability to express oneself.

Chapter 4

Therapy Sessions and School

Therapy Sessions

Albuquerque Therapy Services (ATS) in Albuquerque, New Mexico, has developed a unique approach to serving children with various sensory, motor, and

language needs. As you have noted from reading the previous chapters, these areas of development are often closely related. Although occupational, physical, and speech therapy sessions differ considerably due to the different areas of development that they address, the therapists at ATS operate with very similar philosophies concerning the best ways to help children. Children almost always enjoy the therapy sessions conducted at ATS. Sensory integrative therapy requires that the child direct the session in an environment that the therapist has designed; therapists identify the needs of the child and then design the environment accordingly. Research supports the belief that children will seek out the kind of sensory input they need if appropriate opportunities are available.

Having a variety of environments within a treatment space encourages the child to explore new options when physically and emotionally ready.

Emotional support and encouragement are an important part of therapy.

Children should be encouraged, but never forced, to try to challenge themselves in new ways. Expressions of fear or reluctance must be treated with respect. ATS therapists may try to help children express what is frightening the children or making them uncomfortable to make tasks easier.

Most ATS therapists are also eager to understand and address the reason behind the difficult or unacceptable behavior children sometimes display; the therapists, therefore, will not judge, negate, or belittle children's feelings.

ATS therapists will determine what combinations of sensory-motor experiences (tactile, vestibular, proprioceptive, visual, and auditory) will help the children develop the areas targeted for therapy. Depending on the facilities available, sessions may be conducted in large bright rooms with a wide variety of equipment and movement opportunities, or they may be conducted in small dimly lit rooms with little equipment and a specific movement opportunity. The skilled therapists' choices are limited only by the physical environment. Therapists may also use snacks, drinks, and a wide variety of toys and games in therapy sessions in order to facilitate development and more organized behavior. As children demonstrate understanding, therapy should include education concerning the children's individual sensory needs. Therapists may educate each child individually or, as is the case at Albuquerque Therapy Services, in a small group designed specifically for this purpose. Therapists should prepare the children for this step during earlier therapy sessions through the use of a consistent vocabulary concerning feelings and activities. If your child is currently receiving therapy, you may want to consult with your child's therapists to find out which words they are using.

Therapy conducted with children often relates to their ability to perform academic tasks. Therapy sessions, however, may not look like school and you may question how the activities during a session relate to the academic problems that may have prompted your decision to bring your children to

Some children require a small space in which the therapist can control the combination of sensory input available.

therapy. There may be several answers to your questions, but they usually relate to the fact that children who require therapy may lack certain developmental

Postural support is needed for the focused attention and fine motor abilities necessary for success in school.

pieces. Therapy is often geared toward helping them to fill in the missing pieces, and the activities will support, but not necessarily give your children practice in, academic areas. Some kinds of practice may serve only to frustrate children and cause additional problems in school. When you have questions concerning the ways in which therapy relates to academic success, therapists will do their best to explain them to you.

Most therapists are eager to share the information they have with you. They also need the information you can share with them. Parents have a large pool of knowledge regarding their children's needs and the special ways in which they learn, play, and organize or regulate their own behavior. Many parents do not realize how much they already know about their children's needs in the areas for which the children are receiving therapy. The therapists can use much of your knowledge to help them make therapy more effective, help plan home activities and routines, and make suggestions for the classroom.

Markey (1990) has provided an excellent description of a therapy session conducted with a young child at Albuquerque Therapy Services. Although some of the vocabulary is somewhat technical, the following excerpts (some altered with the permission of the author) may help you to picture a typical therapy session.

Providing an environment in which children can take physical risks encourages this part of normal development.

A Typical Therapy Session

A typical treatment session with J begins in a large treatment room equipped with simple, yet special equipment. Swings, bolsters, slides, therapeutic balls, mattresses filled with water, and mattresses filled with foam comprise some of the equipment used. J is treated by an occupational therapist (Sue) in conjunction with a speech pathologist (Marci). Sue swings J in a linear direction and then adds moderate rotary components to the direction of the swing. This vestibular activity helps J to be at an optimal arousal level for the treatment session.

Next, both J and Sue straddle a big air-filled inner tube (Blackie) and bounce up and down while going round and round. This proprioceptive input helps to modulate J's overactive vestibular system. It is important to encourage heavy work or proprioceptive activities which support J's ability to process both tactile and vestibular input. After J and Sue bounce around the tube, Sue hands J a flash card which pictures the body of an animal. J runs to Marci who has flash cards laid out on the floor picturing the heads of animals. J matches her card to Marci's. Marci says the name and asks J to repeat it. J repeats the name with limited success. J then runs to Sue, mounts Blackie, and starts to bounce up and down and around and around. Marci and Sue encourage J to say "alligator" while she is bouncing. The clarity of the word seems to improve. This bouncing helps to increase the respiratory support for speech.

An aquatic environment can meet a wide variety of sensory and motor needs.

Playing musical chairs was attempted in order to add an auditory component to the activity. Sue and J would bounce as long as the music was playing. The signal for J to pick a flash card and run to Marci was when the music stopped. Adding this component to the activity appeared to be more than J could attend to at one time. This component was omitted.

The flexion swing is the next activity that J chooses. She hangs on to the bolster while Sue swings and bounces. This requires a good flexor pattern. Antigravity flexion is an important component that helps motor planning in early development.

The next activity involves both speech and occupational therapy. After climbing on to a platform, J chooses two colored marking pens to throw to Marci who is sitting on a water-filled mattress. She then swings from the platform on a trapeze. Sue observes that J can pull her knees up toward her chest. This indicates that J is gaining strength in her abdominal muscles. J then releases the trapeze bar and falls into a large soft mattress filled with pieces of foam. The mattress feels like gelatin. The fall provides joint compression, which also activates the joint receptors to increase proprioception for stability and mobility. J then walks across the unstable surface of the mattress, which adds rotational and transitional components of proprioception to the activity.

Postural support provides for improved speech sound production which in turn supports postural mechanisms.

J then sits down with Marci who draws a picture of a cake with candles. She asks J to help blow them out. This blowing helps to increase J's respiratory support for speech. Marci has J repeat words such as "birthday" because multi-syllable words aid in oral-motor planning. J can choose to have candy during the treatment session. Sucking hard candy is believed to aid in flexion components. Chewy, sticky candy aids in the mobility of the oral mechanism involving chewing and tongue lateralization as well as sensory registration. All of these components improve oral-motor skills, which facilitate speech and language development.

As J draws while sitting on the water-filled mattress she receives proprioceptive and tactile input in the upper extremities. Increased input may offer J a fixed-point reference system that allows her to locate herself accurately in the center of her spatial world. It may allow for efficient and effective interpretation of incoming sensory information and planning of outgoing motor information.

J repeats the sequence of climbing on to the platform, choosing markers to throw to Marci, swinging on the trapeze, falling into gelatin, and interacting with Marci several times. This repetition allows for sequencing of events as well as initiating components of praxis.

An ongoing observation of how J reacts to each activity is done by both Sue and Marci. If Sue or Marci recognizes that J is approaching activities in a fearful instead of discriminative way, more vestibular and proprioceptive input is given to attempt to increase organization of tactile and other sensations.

Speech therapy attempts to improve sensory registration, oral-motor planning, mobility of the oral mechanism, and respiratory support for speech. Occupational therapy attempts to improve sensory processing abilities, postural mechanisms, and components of praxis. J's improvement of sensory integrative functions appears to help improve the course of her speech-language acquisition, and her ability to respond adaptively in the areas of speech and language also positively affects her sensory integrative processes. For this reason, speech and occupational therapy are provided jointly.

Therapy in a group allows children to share the process of learning about each individual's sensory needs.

Combined Therapy and Referrals to Other Professionals

Some therapists may recommend that children receive one or more combination therapy sessions a week. A combined therapy session at Albuquerque Therapy Services involves the motor therapist (occupational or physical) and a speech/language pathologist. Both therapists work with children for the entire session using a combination treatment plan designed to capitalize on the way in which sensory motor and speech/language skills depend on one another. These sessions may look different from other motor or speech/language therapies you have observed. They may seem less focused or oriented toward accomplishing a specific task. Experience, however, shows that many children make faster and greater changes in the targeted areas when sensory motor and speech/language treatment are combined. This approach provides reciprocal support for development in each area. An appealing byproduct is that children enjoy the two-to-one attention as well as the different structure of the therapy sessions. If combined therapy is recommended, the therapists will talk with you about the reasons they feel this method is appropriate and will share the treatment plan with you sometime during the first four to six weeks of therapy.

As therapists get to know your children and see how development progresses in various areas, they may identify or suspect a problem in some other area. You may also express concerns that sensory motor or speech/language therapy cannot address. At these times the therapists may refer you to other professionals. Academic and behavior problems are often related to difficulties in sensory processing. These areas may, however, need to be addressed in other ways. In some cases, the progress being made in therapy may be enhanced by additional, specialized services. The therapists may refer you to a counselor or psychologist, a doctor, an audiologist, or an educational diagnostician, or to the available special education services. They may also suggest educational tutoring if there is a very specific area of concern. Therapists frequently seek the advice of other professionals, including a teacher if possible, before making a referral, so you can be assured that the referrals made are based on a consensus of professional opinion. Therapists are frequently acquainted with practitioners in each field who have demonstrated the kind of professional expertise they feel is essential in working with children and can, therefore, suggest an appropriate professional.

School

Although it may sound somewhat redundant, the best schools and teachers are those who can help children learn to love learning. In order to love learning, children must first learn to learn. Learning to learn begins early in life and continues, without much conscious effort, as children mature. This learning, which is the foundation of all other learning, is based, in large part, on the ability to process and use sensory and motor information. An inability to process sensory information adequately will affect learning and, therefore, school performance.

This inability may be quite obvious or it may be difficult to detect. Many children discover, usually without conscious thought, ways to compensate for their difficulties, or differences, in processing information. Other children are not so fortunate and the effects of sensory integrative dysfunction may be manifested in learning and behavior problems at school. A common component of many (some experts say most) learning disabilities, communication disorders, behavior disorders, and mental retardation is an inability to process and use sensory information adequately.

The range of intellectual ability in children with sensory integrative disorders is equal to that of children without disorders. Most are of at least average intelligence; some may be intellectually gifted; others may have intellectual abilities that are below average. For all of these children, however, the most basic demands of the usual school setting, such as the ability to sit still, pay attention, and demonstrate knowledge, may be extremely difficult. They must receive the help they need to process sensory and motor information in order to benefit from the expertise of their teachers. Teachers can give children this help by using the environment, structuring learning tasks, and most importantly, understanding and supporting the children.

The many distractions in a school environment make it difficult for some children to maintain focused attention.

Many teachers sense, and allow for, individual differences without specific information concerning sensory processing. Most others are eager to help children learn and will try to accommodate the needs of their students. It is important that you discuss your concerns about school performance with the principal or school support team as soon as possible. Although most schools are reluctant to honor requests for specific teachers, the school administration will usually try to match children to teachers who are willing and able to meet children's needs.

After your child has been placed in a class, you will probably want to meet with the teacher or teachers to discuss your child's disorder. Appendix B contains suggestions for teachers. You or your child's therapists may want to look through this appendix in order to determine which suggestions will benefit your child. Your child's therapists or an educational consultant employed by the therapists may also be available to meet with school personnel.

A child who has difficulty understanding what is heard may need alternative ways of receiving information.

Chapter 5

Dealing with Children's Emotions

Children's emotions are frequently so intense that it can be somewhat over-whelming for adults. It can be difficult to hold our own emotions in check when we are trying to handle a child whose emotions are out of control. It can also be quite amazing how quickly the child's emotions pass or change. Anyone who spends a large portion of the day with children has probably developed a way, or ways, to help children deal with their emotions. Most of us who care about children understand that their emotions are genuine and should not be ridiculed or negated.

Our own emotions can, however, get in the way of what we know is best. Some of us allow children to express themselves but ignore the underlying problems and hope they go away. We sometimes try to use logic or reason to explain to children why they "shouldn't feel that way." We may assume that an expression of an emotion is intended to get attention and may deal with it as we would other attention-getting behaviors. Regardless of how we respond to children's emotions, and most of us respond in several different ways, we are not always comfortable with ourselves or the message we have given to our children.

Children gain confidence and independence as they learn ways to work through and master immature expressions of their own emotions. When children are able to say "Stop that, I don't like it!" instead of kicking a person who is annoying them, it signifies an important step in learning to take care of themselves and form relationships with others. This is a personal issue and each family must determine the most comfortable way for them to help children deal with their own emotions. There are, however, some general suggestions that may help you to help your child, and yourself, through some growing pains.

As parents, we are often so concerned about our children that we neglect our own needs. But as we have all discovered, usually the hard way, it is difficult, if not impossible, to deal with another person's problems or emotions when we have not taken adequate care of our own. If you are angry or upset over a child's behavior or something else, you must first get control of your own feelings. You may not be able to resolve your feelings over a particular incident in a short period of time, but it is essential to let children know that "I'm feeling too upset (angry, frightened, sad, etc.) right now. I need a little time by myself. I'll talk to you in a minute."

In taking care of our feelings first, we accomplish several things. First, we help children to realize that strong feelings are a fact of life and that everyone must deal with them. Second, adult emotions can be frightening for children and dealing with our own emotions first reassures children that someone will soon be in control. Finally, we set an example for children, and as they see our ability to deal with our own emotions, they gain confidence that they can learn to do the same thing.

If you fail to take care of yourself first, all of your empathy and concern will be forced and most children are quite sensitive to insincere expressions of empathy or concern. In addition, you run the risk of frightening or shaming the child. It is a rare parent who has not made hurtful, judgmental comments about children rather than commenting on the behavior that has caused the anger. It can be a devastating and long-remembered experience to hear a parent yelling such things as "How could you be so stupid? I've told you not to play ball in the house!" Children who are not yet equipped to handle their own emotions are not able to carry an additional burden of guilt or the fear of your emotions.

Children also need to know that someone understands, and cares about, their feelings. Although the things that cause children distress may seem rather petty to us, they are not petty to the children involved. Reflective listening involves hearing a child's feelings and reflecting those feelings back to the child. "You're afraid a monster is going to come out of the closet. It's hard to sleep when you are so worried." This kind of response acknowledges feelings and helps to dissipate the intensity of those feelings. Reflective listening does not indicate that you agree or disagree, only that you understand and care. This is the first step in helping children to deal with their emotions. You must also communicate the expectation that your children will eventually be able to master their emotions.

Having understanding adults who become overly concerned that fearful feelings are too much for children to handle can actually reinforce the very fears that the adults are hoping the children will outgrow. The significant adults in children's lives must have the expectation that children will find developmentally appropriate ways of mastering their fears. A four-year-old may need to take a magic toy to bed to keep the monster away. A nine-year-old may feel less fearful upon discovering that a parent was also afraid of fire drills. Children learn to develop mastery over their emotions in much the same way that they develop mastery of other skills—through learning step by step and practicing. Parents play an integral part in this important process.

In helping children to become increasingly independent, it is important to empower them to handle their own emotions rather than solve the problems for them or control the outcomes. "How can we get your monster under control so you can sleep?" "What do you think you can do, other than scream, when you get mad at your sister?" When you ask questions such as these after acknowledging children's feelings, you help them to take responsibility for dealing appropriately with their emotions. They may need your help in developing strategies, but it is important to expect that they have some input. It is sometimes easy, particularly with children who have disabilities, to focus on problems without the expectation that children will be able to resolve their own problems or assist in the solutions. Doing so, however, will only serve to make the problem worse by creating chronically fearful or angry children who are certain only that they will not be able to solve problems independently.

Young children may be able to use fantasy to overcome emotions. With older children it may be helpful to share your own similar feelings or experiences. Letting them know that elevators (airplanes, snakes, heights, sirens, etc.) make you nervous will help them to recognize that it is normal to experience unreasonable emotions. They may then be better able to develop a sequence of strategies to help them overcome their own fears. Some of these strategies may include adult involvement. If possible, help children to develop other strategies to be used first. You or another adult may become involved if those strategies don't work or if the situation becomes overwhelming to the child involved. An obvious exception is if there is a possibility of danger. For example, a child may be afraid of a bully who calls names and makes fun of others. The child may decide to try ignoring the bully or staying away from the bully. If the bully continues to bother the child or begins to threaten, the child may ask a parent or another adult to talk to the bully or school personnel. Children may feel they have failed if they need to ask for your intervention. In those cases, you may once again need to listen reflectively and help the child to understand that asking for protection, or your intervention, is not a failure but one option in a hierarchy of strategies.

While it is important to acknowledge feelings and help children to deal with them, it is also important to be firm about the limits that you set and help children to understand that their feelings will not necessarily determine the outcome. A child who is afraid to go to school will still have to go to school. A child who is angry over having to do a chore will still have to do that chore. Your responses to those feelings may help to dissipate the intensity of the feelings, and the way you approach the situations may change, but the child's feelings will not change the outcome.

You must also remain firm in the way that you choose to help children deal with their emotions. In some situations and with some children you may need to decide on how much time is appropriate to spend working on solutions. If a child experiences fears in the middle of the night, the best time to develop strategies for dealing with those fears is during the day when everyone is awake and able to think calmly. Then, when the child experiences fears in the night, the parent can listen empathically and remind the child of the strategies they decided on. A frightened child may insist on spending the rest of the night in the parents' bed. If this is not the strategy you decided on, and you are uncomfortable with allowing the child to spend the night in your bed, it is essential to remind the child of that and be firm about the limits that you set.

Parents can usually trust their instincts because they know their children well. If you begin to feel irritable and question whether you are giving in too much or being manipulated, you may want to reevaluate your responses and decide on ways to make yourself feel more comfortable. If you feel the amount of time devoted to dealing with a situation is excessive, you need to express your own needs and then decide on how much time is appropriate. "You get scared in the night and need me to help you get back to sleep. I need to sleep, too. I can spend ten minutes in your room. Then I need to go back to bed. If that's not enough time, you can sleep on the floor in my room, but I need to go to sleep." Children may protest the first time or even the next several times, but if you are firm and respond in the same way each time, they will eventually be able to accept the limits. Some children (and adults) may appear to be experiencing one emotion when the actual emotion is something entirely different. Have you ever watched your child dart across a crowded parking lot? When you reached that child you probably looked and acted as if you were very angry. Were you actually angry or were you afraid? Maybe you were both. In much the same way, it is sometimes difficult to determine what children are feeling. Some children usually appear to be fearful; others usually appear to be angry. It is possible that when children are whiny and clingy, they may actually be angry. Or children may use a show of bravado and power or make hostile defensive comments in order to mask fear and vulnerability. The adults' responsibility is to determine and respond to the primary emotion, not the defenses. Children may need an empathic, reflective response in order to determine which emotion is primary. If you respond reflectively, you will help children to behave in a way that expresses the emotion they are actually feeling.

For example, children who seem fearful, timid, and shy may have had adults consistently respond to them as if they needed someone to protect them, solve their problems, and intervene in their social interactions. When such a child is pushed or cut ahead of in line, the child may look and act helpless. An adult may respond by saying "That scared you!" It would, however, be more empowering for the adult to say "You didn't like that one bit!" This response allows the child to learn a different, more powerful response to the intrusion.

We must all learn that there are appropriate outlets for anger. There are also firm limits on, as well as safe times and places for, the expression of anger. Children must also learn which angry expressions are and are not acceptable and learn that there are appropriate times and places to deal with anger. We also usually know the people in our lives who will hear our anger in a nonjudgmental and caring way and who will not. We must teach our children that it is not emotionally safe to express anger with all people.

You may need to respond empathically and set limits on inappropriate behavior at the same time. "It makes you mad when you get pushed, but you can't hit. Get out of the pool now and we can take a walk and talk about it." In responding this way you are able to empathize, identify the behavior that is not appropriate, say where and when you will discuss the situation, and suggest an appropriate outlet (a walk) for the anger.

Despite our best intentions and efforts, there will be times when children, their parents, or all parties involved temporarily lose control of their emotions. When this happens, it is important to have ways of helping one another to feel better. Children usually know when they have "blown it" and are quite aware of how upsetting their actions can be to adults. They need ways of restoring normal relations. You may ask, "Do you need to do something to feel better about what happened?" Children may need to help to replace something that they have broken or they may want to apologize. Apologies, however, should not be forced. It is easy to learn to fake remorse. Some children may want a hug or to be held after an emotional storm. Other children would prefer to be alone or not to be touched.

Parents and children may both benefit from a short time away from others, especially when inappropriate behavior is, at least in part, due to some amount of sensory overload. All of us are subject to overload from time to time, and there are times when we all need a quiet, nonstimulating environment in order to calm and reorganize ourselves. Children who have difficulty processing sensory information are more prone to become overloaded by some environments or circumstances. When this overload occurs, children benefit from a change in sensory environment.

Be careful not to use this time out as a punishment or your intention to help your child may get lost in the resulting power struggle. It is best to state the need for a time out quietly and calmly. The length of time for the separation should be only as long as children feel it is needed. After the children calm down, they and their parents can briefly talk about what happened and share any leftover feelings.

It is also neither necessary nor desirable to designate a specific time-out place. Children who are placed in a time-out chair for a specific length of time may feel that they have served their time and are free to commit the same misdeed again. Whenever possible, children must be given the opportunity to decide when they can behave well enough to return to the family. For example, the parent of bickering children might say, "You can either stay here and be part of our family dinner, or I must ask you to go eat in the kitchen. I don't like to be around bickering and fighting." Offering children choices helps them learn that it is possible for them to make decisions about their own behavior.

After an intensely emotional situation has passed, you can decide on what you can do the next time it occurs. You may need to decide on appropriate consequences. The consequences, however, should be a result of the behavior, not the emotion. The best consequences are natural. A natural consequence is one that no one imposes, such as, "If you don't come in when you are called for dinner, you will be hungry." When there is no natural consequence that will make an impact, the next best consequences are logical. A logical consequence is one that makes the child responsible for the circumstances arising from the behavior: "If you write on the walls, you will have to clean the walls." An applied consequence is occasionally necessary. Applied consequences are those that do not fit the misbehavior and should be used only when nothing else works: "If you continue to write on the walls even after you have to clean them several times, you may not be allowed to play with your friends" (Guerney 1988).

Emotions are a fact of life and can be very powerful. We all need to know that someone understands our feelings and we must also have ways of dealing with them. A large part of becoming a competent adult is learning appropriate ways of accepting and expressing our own emotions, as well as accepting those of the people close to us. As in all other areas, children need role models who respond appropriately to their emotions.

Chapter 6

Suggestions

Most, if not all, aspects of your child's life are affected to some degree by the sensory integrative disorder for which he or she is receiving treatment. You have probably already discovered many strategies that help your child to feel more comfortable and behave appropriately in various situations. We must, however, make demands from time to time that, although very appropriate and necessary, are hard for children to meet. In addition, there are times when trying to figure out and meet our children's needs can be, at best, frustrating and, at worst, impossible. At those times it is important to remember that, for the most part, children want to do what we want them to do. Children, particularly young children, are anxious to please the people they love. They are, for various reasons, not always able to do so. The same can be said for us as parents. We want to do what is best for our children and patiently provide for their needs. We are not always able to do so. It is important to be as forgiving, supportive, and understanding of ourselves as we are of our children when we are unable to meet one another's or our own expectations.

Children, regardless of disabilities, thrive in an environment that is safe, supportive, and reinforcing, both physically and emotionally. They must learn to accept appropriate limits and meet appropriate demands that may change as they grow and mature. It is in this way that they develop the skills necessary to become confident, productive, independent adults. We must acknowledge and build on their efforts.

Although the same basic rules apply to all children, children with sensory integrative disorders may need some adaptations and additional support. The suggestions offered below are, by necessity, fairly general and many apply to all children. If you have more specific questions please consult your child's therapists.

Helping Children to Get Needed Movement

In the normal developmental sequence and throughout our lives, movement has many functions beyond getting us from one place to another. Babies are driven to move and they use movement to learn about the world. Efficient body movement is one of the primary tasks of childhood (Neill 1987); children need to move to learn. Movement comes before language; it helps us to organize and use the information we receive. Movement reduces stress. Obviously, then, children need to spend much of their waking hours moving in some way.

Because of the ways in which children process sensory information, they are unable to sit still and pay attention; they can do one or the other, but not both. Some children are reluctant to move in ways that help them attend, learn, and participate in many of the activities of life. Other children seem to be in constant motion and yet are unable to accomplish much. The suggestions below are intended to guide you as you seek to help your children move in the ways they need to to calm themselves and focus their attention, or to achieve a more appropriate state of alertness.

It is usually best, particularly as children get older, to tell them why it is important for them to move in various ways. This will help your children to recognize their own needs and discover ways in which they can meet those needs in various situations. You will also want to explain that frequent, short movement breaks are essential since the effect of movement on the nervous system lasts about one half hour. The effect of proprioception, which is one of the most helpful kinds of movement, lasts only about fifteen minutes.

Getting Moving

All of us are reluctant to get moving at times, even when we know it is the best thing for us. Children who are in a low state of arousal are often extremely reluctant to get the movement they need to raise their state of arousal to a more appropriate level. Children who are in a high state of arousal may be reluctant to do the kinds of activities that will be calming for them. In both cases, it is best and easiest to start with some kind of oral activity. In general, chewing is organizing, sucking is calming, and crunching is alerting. Sweet flavors tend to be calming while sour flavors are more alerting and organizing. Hot and bitter flavors are most alerting.

After children begin the appropriate oral activity, you will be better able to persuade them to sit on a large therapy ball and bounce up and down. This activity can be either calming or alerting and can be done while they read, eat a meal, do homework, or do any other activity that seems appropriate for your family. After beginning these activities, children are likely to be more willing to get moving in other ways. Consult with your child's therapists to find out which of the following activities would be most helpful for your child.

Activities

- Most of us benefit from some kind of "wake-up" activity. Waking 15 minutes early for some exercise such as taking the dog for a brisk walk may be helpful and appealing to children. It may also be appropriate for some children to run errands to the local convenience store or to a neighbor's house.

- Any activity that involves hanging by the arms is helpful. You may want to think about getting a chinning bar designed to fit into a doorway or closet. Pushing on walls and jumping up to touch a high point on the wall are also activities that involve using the large joints and muscles in the arms as well as the hips. Throwing or hitting balls or wet sponges against the wall can also be quite helpful.

- Many children enjoy grown-up activities and it will be helpful for them to vacuum, sweep or scrub the floor, push or pull grocery carts (either real or play), or carry items (especially books, grocery bags, light furniture, bricks, watering cans, or other heavy items). Kneading bread or hand mixing pie or cookie dough is helpful. In the absence of the real thing, modeling clay is an excellent substitute. Digging, raking, and hoeing in the garden, watering plants, painting the house with water using big brushes, and washing the car are good outdoor activities.

- Many children benefit from activities that require them to bring their knees to their chests. In addition to somersaults and crawling activities, children may enjoy sitting on the floor, bringing their knees to their chests, and rocking back and forth. A variation of this activity that may be fun at parties is to put a dab of peanut butter on each knee. Children then bring their knees to their mouths to lick the peanut butter off (no hands allowed). Knees may be moved together or separately depending on the child's strength and skill.

- Children usually love to jump, and jumping can be quite helpful for many children. If you are comfortable allowing children to jump on beds or other appropriate furniture, it is an excellent activity. You may also want to sew together two twin bedspreads and stuff them with cubes of foam to make a giant pillow. Some upholsterers are willing to give away scrap pieces of foam. The pillow is wonderful for jumping into and rolling around in. A mini-trampoline, jump rope, or jumping games, such as hopscotch, may be useful for some children but too difficult or not advisable for others. Jumping into a pile of leaves or other textured materials may be fun for some children but distressing to others. Do keep in mind that activities such as jumping on furniture or a trampoline should be carefully supervised to prevent injury.

- When children are involved in sedentary activities such as doing homework, reading, and playing board or video games, encourage them to take frequent, short movement breaks. Sitting on a therapy ball during these activities is also a good idea and can improve their concentration. Insisting that children finish all their homework in one sitting is usually counter-productive.

- Choose family activities that involve appropriate kinds of movement. Children often find doing something with the family more appealing than doing it alone and the whole family may discover new, healthy activities. Walking, swimming, hiking, horseback riding, or playing tennis, baseball, or frisbee are only a few examples of enjoyable family activities.

- Wrestling or other kinds of rough-housing provides sensory input that can be quite intense and, depending on the child, may be very enjoyable or very threatening. For many children, the fun of close rough-housing contact with a parent is very attractive. The sensory input, however, may result in sensory overload, which leaves children in an aggressive state or in tears. The following rules will help to make wrestling a positive experience.
    - No tickling—ever!
    - Allow each person a designated safe spot. When in the safe spot, the wrestler may not be touched by the other wrestler.
    - Allow the child to get away at any time. Feeling trapped may provoke a fright or flight response.
    - The advantage of wrestling is that it provides a lot of heavy work. Pushing, pulling, rolling, and weight-bearing actions are all good. If the child is arching backward frequently, it may be a sign of overload.

- Encourage activities that cause the child to curl up. This kind of movement is more organizing.

- Set a good example by engaging in movement that is helpful for you. Children are more likely to use movement for self-regulation if they see the significant adults in their lives doing the same thing. If you are uncertain about the kinds of movement that are most helpful for you, look carefully at chapter 3. You may want to experiment with different ways to help yourself to relax, concentrate, and maintain an appropriate level of arousal.

- It is usually not a good idea to take away outdoor play privileges as a disciplinary measure. Children need to engage in the kinds of movement they get outdoors. Confining children to a chair, corner, or their rooms for long periods of time can be difficult and frustrating for both parent and child. It is also not effective. If you choose to use time out as a discipline, it should last no longer than five minutes (White, Nielsen, and Johnson 1972) and be followed by some kind of activity that will be helpful for the child. "Helpful" does not necessarily mean fun. If appropriate, scrubbing the kitchen floor may be as useful as playing on the monkey bars.

- Many children, particularly as they grow older, are interested in organized sports of various kinds. These kinds of activities can be very helpful in that they encourage children to enjoy movement and practice certain skills regularly. In addition, some sports encourage the same kind of movement patterns that therapy seeks to develop or enhance.

Most coaches are interested in teaching children sports and skills, and in encouraging them to improve their own performance and to learn to play as a team. In many cases, children learn skills and sports that they can enjoy and use throughout life. Some activities, however, require children to practice skills that they have not yet developed or to stay in the same spot on a playing field for long periods of time while attending to what may be going on in another part of the field. Some organized sports may also require movement patterns that may not be appropriate for children with sensory integrative disorders. In addition, some coaches pressure children to win and may not allow less skilled players to participate very frequently. This attitude can be quite frustrating and possibly counter-productive.

In deciding whether or not to encourage your children to participate in organized sports, consider their strengths and preferences for movement and contact. Some children are threatened by close, unexpected contact and would not, therefore, enjoy soccer, basketball, or other contact sports (tackle football is not usually considered a good sport for young children). Some sports, such as skiing, swimming, and running, do not involve contact and the primary goal is in improving a personal best. These sports may be better choices for some children. Also, ask the coaches about their particular approach to instruction. If possible, observe the coaches in action and try to ensure that your children will be participating in an atmosphere of acceptance and encouragement. Your child's therapist can help you determine which organized sports are best for your child.

Playground Equipment and Additions

Playgrounds and backyards have wonderful potential for all kinds of beneficial movement opportunities. In addition to the standard swings, slides, and jungle gyms, you may want to consider some of the following suggestions to enhance the opportunities available to your children.

- A waterbed mattress filled with water and placed on top of a tarp beneath a swing, rings, or trapeze bar provides additional proprioception that many children crave and almost all enjoy. A mattress can be bought for around $30.00 and should last the summer if you take the precaution of having children remove their shoes before jumping on the waterbed.

- Water play in the summertime provides many opportunities for all kinds of movement. Children will experiment to find the ways they like best. Most children enjoy playing with the hose and running through the sprinklers. Squirting each other or things with various kinds of squirt guns helps to build fine motor skills. Throwing water-filled balloons and wet sponges is also fun. You may want to consider obtaining a shallow, soft-sided wading pool and a long piece of heavy plastic that is constantly wet with a hose so that children can slip and slide.

- Different kinds of swings require different skills and give children needed input. Tire or rope swings and trapezes are a few suggestions.

- A slide can be used in many different ways. Children love to climb up slides as well as slide down. You may want to attach a rope to the top of the slide so that children can grab on to the rope at the bottom and pull themselves up. A rope ladder attached to a tree or climbing structure is also a good addition.

- Children need and benefit from lots of opportunities for pretend play. Large appliance boxes, a pup tent and, if possible, a large cardboard tube provide endless opportunities for movement of various kinds as well as pretend play. Add blankets and a few pieces of lawn furniture for extra fun.

- A sandbox also provides a wide variety of play opportunities. If a large area is not available, consider putting a few pounds of sand into a plastic wading pool with a variety of shovels, sieves, old pans, and cups. Wetting the sand occasionally allows different kinds of input.

Oral Activities

Have you ever heard people joke about not being able to do something unless they hold their mouths just right? As noted before, we all use our mouths to organize, calm, or alert ourselves. Children with sensory integrative dysfunctions need to use their mouths for a wide variety of purposes. There are many activities that you can do easily at home that will help children. Most are fun and require little or no specialized equipment.

- Activities that involve blowing help children to develop the breath support so important for speech and other activities. Many inexpensive whistles and blow toys (party blowers, horns, and kazoos) are readily available. Children may also enjoy blowing table tennis or cotton balls across the floor or a table.

  Blowing bubbles of all kinds is an excellent activity. Children can use straws or tubes to blow bubbles in the bath (with or without bubble bath) or in a sink or tub of water. A small squirt of dish soap will make mounds of bubbles, but make sure children understand the difference between sucking and blowing. A drop of food coloring in the water will also be a big hit. The bubbles and bubble wands available commercially are also fun for children. A less expensive alternative is a bit of dish soap and cornstarch in water. If you want to help the bubbles last longer, add a drop of glycerine (available in drugstores) to the mixture. Cans with the tops and bottoms removed and the edges smoothed out make wonderful bubble blowers. Pipe cleaners twisted into shapes and toy pipes are other fun alternatives.

- Children love to use stickers and sticker books. In order to attach a sticker, children must stick out and move their tongues. This is an excellent oral motor activity. If a child is unable to move his or her tongue to lick the sticker, you may want to move the sticker against the tongue at first. Many inexpensive sticker books are available at toy, grocery, and drug stores. You may also want to keep an eye out for advertising mail containing stickers or address labels. Most of us get a supply of magazine stickers several times a year and children enjoy the bright colors. If you are not too particular, children may also enjoy attaching stamps and address labels and licking and sealing the envelopes. You may want to keep a box full of unwanted return envelopes and stickers for children to play with.

- As noted before, we all use chewing, sucking, and crunching to calm, organize, and alert ourselves. Some children chew on clothing or whatever else is available. Rubber tubing provides a more appropriate alternative if chewing food or gum is not an option. For older children, some erasers or pencil holders that can be bought separately and put onto a pencil are heavy duty enough to take a fair amount of chewing. Make sure that they will not come apart too easily.

  Allowing children to drink with a straw or, even better, out of a sports bottle with a straw attached provides valuable oral stimulation. Drinking pudding, yogurt, kefir, or thick shakes through a straw requires hard sucking that is helpful for many children. (A more complete list of other food suggestions follows.) Do keep in mind that if saliva production (drooling) is an issue, dairy products tend to increase drool and citrus products tend to thin it. Consult with your child's therapists if you have concerns about drooling.

- Different foods have different properties and we all have different needs. You probably already have a good idea of the kinds of foods and food textures that are most helpful for your child. If you have questions about what helps your child to concentrate and reach and maintain an appropriate level of alertness in the therapy setting, ask your child's therapist.

The flavors and textures of foods affect children's ability to calm, organize, and alert themselves. Sweet things have a calming effect. Things that have a sour flavor (a lemon drop or sour ball) are alerting, spicy foods (salsa or cinnamon candies) are more alerting, and bitter and hot foods (jerky or smoked foods) are most alerting.

The movement required to eat foods follows a similar hierarchy. Sucking (on a candy, bottle, or finger) is calming, chewing (on candy, gum, a bagel, or an eraser) is organizing, and crunching (on pretzels, carrot sticks, or a pencil) is alerting. There are many more foods and nonfoods in each area than are in the following list, but the list will help you to come up with more ideas for your family.

Chewy Foods	**Crunchy Foods**	**Sucking Foods**
granola bars	popcorn	hard candy
fruit leather	raw vegetables	frozen novelties
dried fruit	crackers	peanut butter
bagels	pretzels	
cheese	nuts	
gum		

Mealtime

- During mealtimes, make sure that children's feet are flat on the floor and that chairs allow the children to have their elbows at table height. You may also want to put a pillow between the seat back and the child so that the lower back is better supported.

- Allow children to drink through straws.

- Try to include foods that allow children to lick, suck, crunch, and chew. (If licking fingers does not offend you, it is a very good oral activity.)

- Learning to use eating utensils properly can be quite difficult. Insisting on perfection will make mealtimes difficult. It is probably best to compliment children as they come closer and closer to using utensils according to your family's standards. Children are usually eager to please and will improve with time.

- Accidents at mealtimes can be distressing for everyone. If possible, use cups and glasses that are difficult to tip and invest in place mats that prevent dinnerware from slipping on the table. Teach children to take small portions of food in order to minimize spilling and wasting food. Small portions are also easier to manage.

- Help children to reach an appropriate level of alertness *before* the meal begins. It will be hard for children to calm or alert themselves while sitting down to eat. Some children may benefit from sitting on a therapy ball during meals.

Clothes and Dressing

- It is usually best to honor children's clothing preferences. Insisting that children wear certain kinds of clothing may set them up to be easily overloaded and make it difficult for them to attend. What may seem like an insignificant matter to you may seriously affect your child's behavior and comfort. If your child has distinct preferences for certain types of clothing, try to find clothing of those types for all occasions. You will be helping yourself as well as your child.

- Be aware of all the small things that can make clothing uncomfortable. Some children dislike the feel of seams in socks. Seams can also be very uncomfortable if clothes are slightly tight. Stiff labels can be uncomfortable for many of us. You may want to cut the labels out of clothes. If you do this, make a small mark on the inside with an indelible marker to help the child distinguish between front and back. Young children will require a larger, more colorful mark than older children.

  Many children have distinct preferences concerning sleeve length and clothing texture. They may have different texture preferences for tops and bottoms. Turtleneck shirts and shirts with collars may be uncomfortable for some children. Many children dislike tight clothing of any kind; others may prefer tighter clothing and turtlenecks. Some may even like some parts (such as sleeves or socks) to be tight and others (such as pant legs and shirts) to be loose. Be aware of how preferences may change as children mature or as therapy progresses.

- Helping children to dress appropriately for the weather can be challenging. Many children who have difficulty processing sensory information dislike wearing hats, coats, and gloves. If children object to wearing coats, it is sometimes helpful to allow them to dress in loose layers. If hats and gloves are absolutely essential, allow children to try them on and choose the ones that are most comfortable.

  It is also helpful to remember that we tend to dress children according to how *we* perceive the temperature. Children who are tactilely defensive may actually be warmer than most people and can easily become overheated. In many cases children are more able to determine appropriate clothing for themselves than we may imagine. Most children, unless they are unable to register temperature effects on the body, will not allow themselves to become too uncomfortable.

- If getting children dressed in the morning is a problem, consider allowing them to dress while they are still in a sleeping bag or under the covers. If you need to help your child get dressed, remember that he or she may be averse to light touch. Many children also dislike being completely uncovered. Try removing and replacing one item of clothing at a time. As often as possible, allow enough time for children to help to dress themselves.

Being allowed to suck on a drink bottle or chew on something while dressing may help some children. An appropriate snack or a few minutes of outside play following dressing may help to motivate children to dress. Some children may also be more willing to dress if allowed to watch TV or listen to music during or immediately after dressing.

Bedtime Routines

- A warm bath is an excellent way to help children to relax for bed. You will want to help children to keep the water temperature constant during the bath. A few minutes of water play, particularly blowing bubbles, is both fun and helpful. Older children may prefer a shower. This can be relaxing or alerting. You probably know whether or not a shower at bedtime is appropriate. Bath sheets or beach towels are wonderful for wrapping children in after the bath or shower. Dressing for bed while still in the bathroom is usually a good idea.

- Almost everyone benefits from having a little time to relax and unwind before going to sleep. For younger children, establish a routine of reading a story, singing songs, listening to quiet music, or having a conversation before you leave the room. You may also want to leave a box of quiet toys for children to play with before going to sleep. Some children may benefit from a back rub, being rocked, or being tucked in or wrapped up. Older children may enjoy having a small light they can turn off (without getting out of bed) after a short period of reading or listening to music.

- Children may benefit from different kinds of bedtime environments. Depending on your child's preferences, you may want to consider flannel sheets, an indoor sleeping bag, a waterbed, a bed tent, or additional pillows at the head or around the sides of the bed.

- It is usually best to honor preferences for lighting. Bulbs of various wattages can be used in many night lights or small lamps. If children insist on having bright lights on as they go to sleep and this presents a problem for you, consider lowering the wattage of the light bulbs in the room over time.

Chores and Homework

- Before insisting that a child perform various tasks, make sure the task is appropriate for the child. Unfortunately, we do not always have accurate perceptions of what our children are able to do. Parents and teachers may make the mistake of assigning tasks to children who have not yet acquired the necessary skills to complete them. For example, greasing the car or practicing calculus would not be good assignments for me since I have not acquired the skills needed to perform them. We also may not be willing to accept our children's performance of a task if they did not do it to our standards. If one of your child's chores is making a bed and you always fix it, the child will probably lose the motivation to do the task.

- If children are unable to complete chores or assignments, or if they do them incorrectly, consider the possibility that they did not adequately understand what was required of them. It is sometimes easy to assume that children do not do chores correctly because they want to escape from the responsibility when, in fact, they think they have done what you asked. I once asked my son to put a large trash bag in the can and then empty the trash. When I later went outside, I discovered that he had emptied the trash on top of, not in, the large trash bag. While I was reprimanding him, he said, "But, Mom, I did what you said. I put in a big trash bag first."

- Make chores and homework a part of the daily routine. It is easier to remember a task if it is performed at the same time each day. When deciding on a schedule, keep in mind children's likes, dislikes, and their best time of day. They may not feel particularly cooperative if you ask them to perform chores during their favorite TV program. If it doesn't matter when the chores are done, ask children whether they would prefer to do them first thing in the morning, after school, or at some other time that fits your family's routine.

- Break chores and homework up into small, manageable pieces. Children sometimes feel overwhelmed by what appears to them to be an enormous amount of work. Schedule small breaks when they complete part of the task. Encourage children to participate in some kind of movement during break times: "After you finish the first ten problems, you can ride your bike for 15 minutes." This movement will enhance their ability to concentrate when they return to the task.

  Children who are able to work continuously for several minutes may respond well to the use of a timer. "You can work on your spelling for fifteen minutes and then take a break to play outside." If you choose to do this, make sure your child is actually able to work for the majority of the time period. Some children may not have a clear enough concept of how long they must work and may spend most of the time wondering when the timer is going to go off.

- Some chores are more appropriate than others in terms of their movement components. Jobs that require refined movements and inadequate heavy work such as dusting, pulling small weeds, or doing dishes may not provide children with the kinds of movement most helpful to them. They will not be able to complete such chores successfully.

- Allow children the support they need to perform various tasks. Many people like to have something to eat or drink while they are working. The ability to concentrate and perform may be enhanced or inhibited by the child's body position, lighting, colors, and various other factors in the environment. Some children may work better while seated on a ball; some may be better able to concentrate curled up in a corner with pillows and blankets. Some children need relative quiet in order to do homework, while others benefit from having some music or other noise. What is traditionally thought of as a good working environment may not be an atmosphere in which your child is able to complete tasks efficiently. You probably have a good idea of what helps your child to concentrate, but if you are unsure, you may want to experiment with different positions, physical environments, and so forth. Your child's therapist may also have some good ideas for you.

- It is sometimes helpful to remember that very few of us work hard for long periods of time for the sheer joy of working. Some children may work better if there is a specific goal in mind. Younger children often enjoy putting stars or stickers on a chart as a measure of the tasks they have successfully completed. Older children may want some kind of back-up reinforcement on a periodic basis. There are many books that have excellent suggestions on how to set up chore and homework charts (Becker 1971; Rosemond 1989; Garber et al. 1989, are some examples).

In general, if you choose to use charts or other reinforcement, it is a good idea to use privileges and activities rather than money or objects as a reward. As adults, we earn things other than money for contributing to the smooth functioning of the household. Children should also be expected to contribute without a constant monetary reward.

It is not unreasonable to suggest that children earn television hours or minutes on the video game. Allowing children to choose a family game, activity, outing, or a special event to attend can also reinforce their completing tasks. The longer the time period required to complete the activity, the more points, stickers, and so on the child will earn. You and your child may occasionally decide to allow him or her to work for some special item. This, however, should be the exception rather than the rule.

Outings and Travel

At times, we all want or need our children to participate in activities that require them to sit relatively quietly for long periods of time. This can be difficult for some children. The following suggestions are intended for those times.

- Prior to the event that will require the child to sit quietly (religious services, dinner at a restaurant, airplane travel, and so on), encourage as much movement as possible. This movement will help children who are in a high state of alertness to be calm and will help children who are in a low state of alertness to attend.

- If at all possible, allow children to take frequent wiggle breaks. On a long car trip, it is good for everyone to get out of the car and move around at least once an hour. It is also advisable to get up and walk around a plane or train at least as often. During religious services or performances of various kinds, teach children to brace their arms and push themselves out of their seats, holding this position for a few moments. Also, make sure that children take advantage of every opportunity to stand or actively participate in the event.

- Always try to think of some kind of oral stimulation that may be appropriate in various situations. While traveling, you will want to have a variety of crunchy and chewy snacks as well as hard candy or suckers. Once again, a sports bottle with an attached straw is indispensable. If obvious snacking is not appropriate, allow children to chew gum or suck on small hard candies. Some children may benefit from having a length of rubber tubing to chew.

- Small cushions that can be filled with water or air are often available at sporting events or sporting goods stores. These cushions provide a slightly unstable surface to sit on that allows children to get some needed movement. You may want to invest in one or two to have on hand for when you need your children to sit quietly.

- It may be helpful for children to have small, quiet hand toys to play with. Sensory balls, worry stones, a small lump of play putty or molding dough, and erasers of various shapes are all possibilities. Some children may even enjoy different kinds of fabric squares. If you watch your children for awhile you will probably discover other possible toys.

- Allow children to dress comfortably. If a certain style of dress is mandatory, spend some time prior to the event helping your child find appropriate clothing that is still comfortable. Children will be better able to tolerate other kinds of sensory stimulation or lack of stimulation if they are not unduly irritated by clothing.

Organization

Children who do not adequately process sensory information or who have trouble with one or more of the various aspects of praxis often have a difficult time organizing themselves to perform the many tasks required of them. It is therefore little wonder that they are unable to organize their rooms, possessions, and desks or lockers at school. To a certain extent, this lack of organization must be dealt with primarily through patience. There are, however, a few ideas that may make life a little easier for both parent and child.

- As you probably discovered while reading chapter 3, we all have different ideas concerning the best way to organize personal environments. Most of us arrange our children's possessions according to our own view of how it should be done. As children get older, they may develop different ideas. It will be helpful for you to spend some time with your children in their rooms to find ways to organize possessions that are acceptable to you both. If children have a say in the way things are organized, they may be more willing to maintain that organization.

- Use containers that are accessible and easy for children to use. The original packaging of toys, crayons, and so on, are rarely acceptable for long-term use. Many families place boxes or baskets, cloth bags, coffee cans, and empty milk or other containers on low shelves or easily opened drawers. Color coding or labeling containers with words or pictures may also be helpful. Smaller containers can be used in desks or work spaces.

- You may want to find small pictures of socks, underwear, and so forth, that you can put on drawers or other storage spaces. Using the pictures for a guide, children are better able to find and put clothing away independently.

- Younger children may benefit from being able to find clothing stored as outfits rather than individual pieces of clothing. They can then satisfy themselves by picking out their own clothes and satisfy you by having a well-coordinated outfit.

- Being able to hang jackets, pajamas, backpacks, towels, and washcloths on hooks rather than hangers is easier and more appealing to children. You may be more successful in keeping things off the floor and furniture if you buy a few decorative hooks to use in the bedroom, bathroom, and kitchen.

- Many of us use lists, calendars, or other reminders to help us remember assignments and appointments. Children will benefit from learning to use similar strategies at an early age. You can start by using pictures with very young children. You may then progress to using one-word notes until children are able to use such reminders independently. You can use notes to help children remember the chores they need to do and events they need to attend. You will probably want to include things that children enjoy so that they do not learn to avoid lists of things to do.

You can help children remember class assignments by creating an assignment card (see the example below). If children have a hard time remembering to write assignments down, ask the teacher to initial the assignment card at the end of each period or the end of the day.

Assignments

Date _____

Initial	Subjects	Is there an assignment?		What is it?
_____	Math	Yes	No	_____
_____	Reading	Yes	No	_____
_____	Social Studies	Yes	No	_____
_____	Science	Yes	No	_____

- Use routines to help children avoid losing things and rushing. If it is routine for them to place items they need at school the next day in a specific spot, children are less likely to forget them or be in a hurry. In the same way, children who are encouraged to put shoes, jackets, and so forth, in the same spot every time they take those items off are less likely to have a hard time finding those items.
- Learning to use a timer will help children to organize their time. It will also help children who have a hard time ending activities to know that they have a specific amount of time to finish the activity and then they will be expected to stop. A bonus of using a timer is that children often transfer the responsibility of ending the activity or sending them to bed from you to the timer.

Communication

Learning to communicate with others is one of the primary tasks of childhood. We use communication for several purposes: to direct or request, to get help or information, to show and share, to label, and to interact. Children must learn, primarily from the people they live with, how to use communication for all these purposes. Communication within a family is essential from many standpoints and it can be extremely frustrating and stressful if the people within a family are unable to communicate effectively. Communication involves both the ability to initiate a conversation and the ability to respond when another initiates it. As you have discovered from reading the previous chapters, communication is extremely complex and can be difficult for children with sensory integrative disorders. Once again, it is important to be understanding and forgiving of one another and willing to try new ways when the old ways fail.

There are many excellent books written about communication and helping children to learn to use language. If you have further questions or concerns about this topic, please refer to the bibliography. If your child has an identified communication disorder, you will want to consult your child's speech and language pathologist for specific recommendations.

- In order for children to learn to use language effectively, it is usually a good idea to *almost* match your use of language to theirs. The level of language you use with young children should be one step ahead of the level of language they are using. For example, if children are using two-word sentences, you would want to use three-word sentences. When you use a word that is unfamiliar to your child, try to make sure the child understands the meaning of the word and then use it again several times to help him or her understand how it is used.

- When children are under stress for any reason, it is best to use simple language and short sentences. Children who are upset or having a difficult time dealing with the demands of the moment are unable to understand long, complex discussions or explanations. In addition, because language places so many demands on the nervous system, too much language can further overload children and cause even greater stress. Adults who understand this concept are sometimes questioned about talking down to children. It is, however, more a matter of using appropriate language for the situation. There is a time to help children learn to use more advanced language and a time to go back to simpler means of communication.

- Taking turns is an important aspect of communication that is sometimes difficult for children with sensory integrative disorders to learn. "Peek-a-boo" is one of the games that helps babies to learn about taking turns. Both adult and baby take turns hiding their faces, each allowing the other time to hide and come out of hiding. Children with sensory integrative disorders may not respond as quickly as other children in this or other games and may, therefore, lose their turn. If this happens often enough, children have a hard time learning to take turns in communication.

It is important for an adult to give children of all ages *enough time* to take a turn in communication as well as in the many other situations that require people to take turns. Waiting can sometimes become uncomfortable, but it is important to give the children a chance to complete their turns before "filling in the blank," doing something for them, or turning away to do something else.

There are many ways in which we can help children learn to take turns. Young children love to play all kinds of games that involve doing something and then allowing an adult to do the same thing. An example is stacking blocks. When children get a little older, they enjoy taking turns with drawing or coloring pictures, naming pictures in a book, sliding down a slide, saying nursery rhymes, being "it," saying color words or names of animals, and eventually playing more structured games.

- Give one instruction at a time until it is clear to you that the child can handle more. Then give only two at a time and slowly add more. It is also important to make sure that children understand the instructions. Ask them to repeat what they are supposed to do. Praise children when they ask questions or ask you to repeat things. They are trying to make sure they understand. Recognizing what they don't know or understand is an important step.

- Make sure that children are attending to you before speaking. You may have to wait until they finish what they are doing or ask them to stop while you talk to them. It is sometimes difficult for them to attend to two or more things at the same time.

- Some children have a difficult time learning the social rules of language. Try not to be too embarrassed when children fail to use these rules. You may need to help children learn by explaining to them what people expect. For example, some of us are able to attend very well without looking at a speaker. It is, however, more acceptable to make eye contact with the person who is speaking. It may be helpful to explain to children that "people need to see your eyes." Other rules or customs may also need to be explained.

- If children have a hard time using facial expression to communicate you may want to help them by asking them to "show me with your face." This, however, may be extremely difficult for some children.

- We are all guilty of asking silly questions from time to time. "Who do you think you are?" or "What do you think you're doing?" are questions every child has heard and few have been able to answer. Children take most of what we say very literally and it is not until they acquire very advanced language skills that they understand that not every question is meant to be answered. Humor, especially sarcasm, can also be difficult for children to understand. If your family enjoys joking, help children to understand the humor by using gestures and facial expressions. You may also ask such questions as, "Is that silly?" It is usually best not to use sarcasm until children are able to understand. Even with older children you may want to ask, "Do you think he really means that?" or "What do you think I really mean?"

- Children may need you to interpret what unfamiliar people say to them. It is sometimes difficult for them to understand a different voice or way of speaking. It is easy to assume that they are ignoring someone when actually they may not understand what is being said.

Bibliography

Ayres, J. A. 1979. *Sensory integration and the child*. Los Angeles: Western Psychological Services.

Becker, W. C. 1971. *Parents are teachers*. Los Angeles: Research Press.

Faber, A., and E. Mazlish. 1974. *Liberated parents, liberated children*. New York: Avon.

Garber, S. W., M. D. Garber, and R. F. Spizman. 1989. *Good behavior*. New York: Villard Books.

Greenspan, S., and N. Greenspan. 1985. *First feelings*. Dallas: Penguin Books.

Guerney, L. F. 1988. *Parenting, a skills training manual*. State College, PA: Institute for the Development of Emotional and Life Skills.

Laurel, M., and P. Elledge. 1985. Time-sampling procedure for assessing communication in adult-child interactions. Paper presented to the American Speech-Language-Hearing Association, Washington, DC.

Markey, R. 1990. Sensory integrative dysfunction: A case study. Senior research project, University of New Mexico.

Meacham, J. 1979. Role of verbal activity in remembering the goals of action. In *Development of self regulation through private speech*, edited by E. Zivin. New York: Wiley.

Neill, L. P. 1987. *Sensory integration and the classroom teacher*. Paper presented at Professional Development Program Workshop, Albuquerque, NM.

Oetter, P. In press. *A treatment planning guide*. Hugo, MN: Professional Development Publications.

Painter, M. 1977. Fluorescent lights and hyperactivity in children: An experiment. *Academic Therapy* 2(12):181-84.

Pearce, J. C. 1980. *Magical child: Rediscovering nature's plan for our children*. New York: E.P. Dutton.

Richter, E., and P. Oetter. 1990. Environmental matrices for sensory integration. In *Environment: Implications for occupational therapy practice*, edited by S. C. Merrill. Rockville, MD: The American Occupational Therapy Association.

Rosemond, J. 1981. *Parent power! A common-sense approach to raising your children in the eighties*. New York: Pocket Books.

_____. 1989. *Six-point plan for raising happy, healthy children*. New York: Andrews and McNeel.

Stilwell, J. M., T. K. Crowe, and L. W. McCallum. 1978. Postrotary nystagmus duration as a function of communication disorders. *American Journal of Occupational Therapy* 32:222-28.

Turecki, S. 1985. *The difficult child*. New York: Bantam Books.

White, G. D., G. Neilsen, and S. M. Johnson. 1972. Timeout duration and the suppression of deviant behavior in children. *Journal of Applied Behavior Analysis* 5:111-20.

Wilbarger, P., and J. L. Wilbarger. 1991. *Sensory defensiveness in children, age two to twelve: An intervention guide for parents and other caretakers*. Santa Barbara, CA: Avanti Educational Programs.

Windeck, S., and M. Laurel. 1989. A theoretical framework combining speech-language therapy with sensory integration treatment. *Sensory integration special interest section newsletter* 12(1).

Appendix A:
Helpful Items

You may find the following items useful to have in your home or at school for your children. Although I have described some of them in the text, I include the items here for easy reference.

- A therapy ball, available at medical supply houses or educational materials stores, makes a good seat for doing homework, watching television, or playing games. Different sizes are available for different aged children. If you want the ball to stay put rather than roll around, set it on an inner tube (size 15 or 16).

- A large cushion made of two pieces of fabric (at least 6 feet by 4 feet; two twin-size bedspreads work well if you have the room) sewn together and stuffed with chunks of foam is wonderful for jumping into. Chunks should be about four inches square. Upholstery shops may save scraps of foam for you.

- Some building supply outlets have heavy cardboard tubes that are used as forms for concrete pillars. The tubes come in various widths and can be cut to specific lengths. A 6- or 8-foot length is wonderful for play.

- Heavy pillows can be used for pillow fights, to cozy up in a corner, or to lie under or on top of.

- A loofah sponge in the shower may help to increase alertness.

- A variety of whistles and blow toys is very helpful when children need some kind of oral activity.

Appendix B: Suggestions for Teachers

The demands that we place on children in school can make the world a rather frustrating place for children with sensory integrative disorders. Our goal as teachers, however, is to help children to learn all that they can and to give them the skills necessary to sort things out, to use various objects, and to function effectively in a complex world.

Basic to the work that we do with children should be the knowledge that, for the most part, children want to do what we want them to do. Children, particularly young children, are eager to please the significant adults in their environment. For various reasons they are not always able to do so. Our job is to provide them with a physically and emotionally safe, supportive, and reinforcing environment that will allow all our students to be valued and accepted for who they are. By acknowledging and building on their efforts we can help them to develop the strategies and skills necessary to become secure, happy, and productive adults.

In order to reach this goal, we need to make some adaptations for children with sensory integrative disorders. (Keep in mind that children may have more than one type of sensory integrative dysfunction.) Some of these suggestions may seem quite obvious to you, while others will be impossible to implement in your classroom. Do, however, give some careful consideration to adaptations you may be able to make in your classroom for those students who need a little extra something. Many of the suggestions offered below will be helpful for all students.

Activities

- Allow children to get up and move around the room, go to the bathroom, or get a drink when they are doing seat work. When you first introduce this idea, there may be some minor chaos but the novelty will soon wear off.

- Do some wake-up activities before starting instruction. Long bus rides to school are not conducive to high levels of alertness. Some calisthenics, movement to music, running, and jumping in place are all good. Similar activities can be used for a minute or two throughout the day whenever you sense the need.

- Include movement in instruction as much as possible. With a little creativity, beanbag tosses, relays, treasure hunts, and obstacle courses can be used to reinforce learning in most areas.

- Make sure that children do not just sit or wander around during recess. It should be a period of strenuous activity. Running, swinging, sliding, and hanging or climbing on the monkey bars are all activities that help children organize themselves.

- Keeping children in for recess as a consequence of not getting work done is counter-productive. It creates a cycle that is hard to break. Children who do not finish their work and are not allowed to move in ways they need will be less likely to finish the work. If you feel strongly about providing a consequence, give those children who do finish their work five extra minutes of free time. You may also consider sending children who have not finished their work out to run a lap around the playground. They must return to the classroom to finish their work.

- Allow children, particularly those who need the movement, to run messages to the office or other teachers, carry books, or move furniture. It is sometimes helpful to keep one or two stacks of heavy books that need to be taken periodically to another teacher across campus. The two teachers can agree to use this strategy for students who need heavy work.

- Allow children to write on the chalkboard before writing on paper. The large movement of trunk, shoulders, and arms will facilitate the posture, control, and feedback necessary for this fine motor task.

- Some children may be better able to work if allowed to stand by a high counter or bookshelf. Also, many children benefit from sitting on a large therapy ball, which allows them to get the movement they need while working (see Appendix A).

- It may be difficult for some children to sort out all the visual, auditory, and tactile stimuli in a classroom. Allowing them to work in a study room may help them. It may also be too challenging for some children to work close to others. Consider allowing them to stand or sit slightly away from, behind, or with their backs to the rest of the group. This strategy will help to cut out excess stimuli.

Scheduling/Seating

- Schedule activities in such a way that periods of sitting are alternated with periods of movement.
- Activities that require fairly intense concentration (reading, math, language) should ideally follow P.E., recess, or therapy, if the child receives therapy.
- Try to schedule a change in activities frequently. Fifteen minutes can be a long time for children to concentrate.
- Children who are easily distracted should be seated in the quietest part of the classroom, away from noise, bulletin boards, and so on. Children who have a hard time staying focused and on task should be seated near the teacher.

Language

- Many children will have some difficulty attending to advanced language and learning a new skill at the same time. If you are teaching new math concepts (or any others), use fairly simple language so that, during math period, math is the challenge, not language.

- Give one instruction at a time to begin with. As children become able to follow one-step instructions, go to two-step instructions, then three-step instructions, and so on.

- Some children learn more easily using their vision. These children will best be able to follow written instructions (words, pictures, diagrams). Others will be better able to follow verbal instructions.

- If children have difficulty following directions, ask them to repeat instructions in their own words. Also, reinforce these children for asking you to repeat instructions or to clarify instructions. Consider allowing children to consult with their neighbors. Other children can sometimes explain better than we can.

- Make sure children are attending to you before speaking. You may have to wait until they finish what they are doing or interrupt them. It is often difficult to listen and do something else at the same time. You can help children who have trouble attending by standing close and putting a hand on their shoulders while explaining.

- Using simple language, make your expectations clear before beginning. Explain the activity and the behavior you expect during the activity.

- Keep instructions as simple and specific as possible.

- Demonstrate as much as possible while explaining.

- Do not ask rhetorical questions or use sarcasm. Children may take you literally. When you use humor, help the children to understand by using gestures and facial expressions. Also ask questions such as "Does that make sense?"

Touch

- Use firm pressure when touching children. Never use light touch. Pats on the head, back, or shoulder are not reinforcing for children with tactile system dysfunction. Straight, downward pushes on the top of the head or on both shoulders are calming for many children. A heavy bear hug is also excellent. Be sure the child is expecting your touch; never surprise a child.

- Do not tickle children or touch their hair during play. This can provide unpleasant stimulation.

- Avoid touching or approaching children from behind. Make sure children see you before giving instructions or asking for responses.

- When using physical prompts, instructions, or guidance, use as firm a touch as possible without hurting.

Equipment

- Children can sit on large therapy balls that have been inflated to chair height. They are available in different sizes for different aged children. A size 13 or 14 inner tube can be placed under the ball to keep it from rolling. Children can also sit in inner tubes on the floor. You can use inner tubes for small group sessions. Larger inner tubes are fun for sitting and bouncing on.

- Heavy pillows are great for the reading corner. They can also be used as punching bags, and some children will benefit from having the pillows piled on top of them. This activity provides proprioceptive input. Old T-shirts stuffed with kapok or some other heavy stuffing material and sewn shut are popular with children.

- A rocking chair is wonderful for students and teachers. Check to make sure the chair you want to put in your classroom will meet the fire code.

- Large cardboard tubes (used for constructing concrete pillars) are useful for crawling through, rolling over, and resting in. They come in different diameters and lengths. A tube that is eighteen inches in diameter is most versatile.

- A freestanding dome tent will provide a place for overstimulated or fearful children to withdraw for short periods of time. It can also be used for one-to-one instruction and small, quiet groups.

- A small plastic wading pool filled with pinto beans can be used in several ways. Many children enjoy sitting in the pool and pouring the beans over their heads, arms, and legs. This activity provides the deep input that many children crave. Puzzle pieces, flash cards, picture cards, or small items for naming or other language activities can be hidden in the beans. Finding the items provides valuable tactile and proprioceptive input. (You may need to supervise the pool closely, depending on the ages of your children; young children can suffocate or choke on pinto beans.)

- Sandpaper and shallow trays filled with clay or wet sand are useful for all kinds of writing activities.

- Study carrels come in various sizes and can be purchased or made from cardboard or plywood. In order to be most useful they should be placed in such a way that they eliminate visual stimuli from both sides.

Environments

- Researchers (Painter 1977) have concluded that fluorescent lighting is detrimental to students who are hyperactive. If there is adequate natural lighting in your classroom, consider turning off the fluorescent lights. If not, you may want to use some incandescent lamps. Once again, check fire codes before bringing lamps to school. If it is impossible to eliminate the fluorescent lights, turn on only the number necessary and turn them off periodically when children need calming.

- While it is important to have a stimulating classroom environment and displays that allow for incidental learning, it is also important to provide an area without excess visual stimuli. Some children may need to use this area for seat work. Areas for group instruction (reading table, and so forth) should be placed away from doors, windows, or heavy traffic areas. Children should not be facing bulletin boards or anything else that will be visually distracting.

- Provide a quiet, soft, comfortable corner or tent that children can use as needed. It should be softly lit and filled with pillows and soft blankets. Stuffed animals are a nice addition for young children. Many children can calm themselves if given the place and opportunity to do so. This area should not be used for disciplinary time out or for play. It can, however, be used for one-to-one instruction.

- Soft music may be calming for some children and distracting to others. Experiment with ways of using headsets for those children who benefit from it.

Behavior Management

- Reinforce children who are behaving appropriately. The others will frequently follow along.

- Do not insist that children can perform if they want to or if they try harder. Doing so can only frustrate children and cause them to have low self-esteem. Most often the accusations are not true.

- Reinforce *small* improvements in behavior so you can help students behave better in time. For example, if certain children complete only two items on an assignment before their minds start to wander, ask them to complete three items and then give them immediate reinforcement if they are successful. After a few days of success, you can increase the number to four. Do not expect consistent performance at first. Some days are bound to be better than others.

- Remember that you cannot take away a behavior without replacing it with another similar, noncompatible behavior. Finding replacement behaviors can be very challenging, but it is an important principle of behavior management as well as an appropriate instructional strategy for students with a sensory integrative disorder. For example, if a child makes annoying oral noises, reinforce the child for chewing gum quietly or sucking on hard candy. These are appropriate oral behaviors that are incompatible with making noises.

- Allow students to experience the logical consequences of their behavior. If they play appropriately at recess, reinforce the behavior by giving them additional opportunities for play. If they make a mess in the rest room, have them clean the rest room during the next recess; don't have them sit in the classroom.

- Many students who have behavior problems as a result of sensory integrative or other disorders follow a pattern of behaviors before they "blow." Other students can be expected to behave inappropriately in certain situations (lunchroom, assemblies, transitions). If you are aware of these patterns of behavior, try to think of ways you can break the pattern *before* the child loses control. You might want to send the child to the playground to do some heavy work or find some heavy lifting, pushing, or pulling for him or her to do around the school or in the classroom. If an occupational or physical therapist is available and willing, arrange for the child to go with the therapist to receive the needed input.

  Give the child advance notice when difficult situations are coming up. Allow the child to walk at the beginning or end of the line or to sit alone or at the back of the room. Ask "What will help you in this situation?" Ask if the child needs to calm down in the quiet corner. When children learn to ask for what they need, they are taking important steps in learning to control their own behavior.

- It is sometimes easy to ignore quiet children who never disrupt the class. Be aware that these children may have problems at least as serious as those who require constant attention.

- Dealing with children who cannot easily control their own behavior can be quite exhausting. Seek out a support system in your school. Perhaps another teacher would be willing to trade duties with you for short periods of time. If children can perform certain tasks, they may be allowed to help the P.E. instructor or cafeteria workers. Therapists may be happy to have a child run errands or move materials. Parent volunteers, if carefully directed, can also be quite helpful. Take care to reduce your own stress as much as possible. An overloaded adult is probably the worst person to deal with an overloaded child.

Overcoming Fear

- Children with sensory integrative disorders may be afraid to perform unfamiliar tasks or activities. Let them watch others perform the task or activity.

- Do the activity with the child using firm touch (for example, go down the slide while holding the child).

- Give children the option of trying *one* time and then allow them to choose not to continue if they do not want to participate.

- If children are resistive or demonstrate extreme reluctance in other ways, do not attempt to force them to participate. Children often know what is best for them.

Other Suggestions

- We all use our mouths to organize ourselves. Think about how many times a day you put your hand to your mouth or put something in your mouth. Many children will be better able to concentrate and have a more appropriate level of alertness if they are allowed to chew gum (large wads are best—sorry!) or suck on hard sour candy. You may want to consider making containers available that are filled with gum, hard sour candy (sugarless is fine), or pretzels or some other hard, crunchy foods. You may also consider allowing children to sip water from individual sports bottles (the ones with large, attached plastic straws) throughout the day.

  If you use food as a reinforcement, you can allow children to earn various food items. Make sure there is plenty of opportunity to earn the items. You may need to make some items, sour candy for example, noncontingent. This concept may cause some initial disruption, but eventually the children who need it will be the ones who use it most.

- Children may have a hard time knowing where to start when presented with an entire page of written material. Teach them how to use a cardboard mask to block out all but a few lines at a time. Writing math problems on graph paper may help some children to organize the columns of numbers.

- Children often need demonstration as well as verbal direction. Complex activities can be broken down into small tasks and then chained together. Children will benefit from your feedback about their success so they will know what a correct pattern feels like.